The Leather lace Bullwhip

A pictorial guide

Copyright © 2011 Paul Carpenter

Geared mainly to the

leather hobbyist with some

braiding experiance,

This book will show you

how to make a cowhide bullwhip

in my unique way.

Published by Lulu.com

ISBN number 978-1-4478-8556-6

Other publications by Paul Carpenter

Travel;

Six Mountain hikes from around the World

The Moray way and the Ben Macdui Trail

Crafts;

Leather and Wood Crafts

Bows and Arrows, Homemade

Leather Armour

Leather Projects

Contents

Materials and tools……..7

Day 1 – lace prep – cutting lace – bevel lace – taper lace – dyeing lace – handle and inner core – top and transition knots   9

Day 2 – braid 1st inlay plus extended core – pulling lace – breakages – rolling - binding – making the Fall – string - strap (optional)……..25

Day 3 – braid 2nd and final inlay – handle braid – 12 to 10 – 10 to 8 – 8 to 6 – 6 to 4 – attach fall and string – final rolling – fix on both knots + strap……..51

Appendix – Lace cutting lengths for 3ft, 5 ft, 8 ft and 9ft bullwhips – possible braid patterns……..81

Pineapple knots……..87

Resources……..91

As always, the procedures outlined within this book you do at your own risk involving the use of sharpo instruments and chemical (colour dye).

The Leather lace Bullwhip

This tutorial is more for the complete beginner with some braiding experience. The techniques and methods I use have developed after intensive help from better and more productive Whipmakers such as Tony Layzell and the late Ron Edwards, these methods I use differed greatly in some respects and are similar in most having over time got used to methods that are possible with the limited amount of skill and tools I have at hand – in other words, if I can make whips, so can anybody.

This tutorial will be based over three days giving you the time needed in learning the skills and concentration needed while braiding, I still take three days with some whips – I am left handed so some instructions may need to be reversed by right hander's. It is probably best to read the whole tutorial first before proceeding.

This is the finished 6 ft bullwhip and a stock whip I made for this tutorial.

Materials and tools

These are the main materials and tools needed to make a whip. There are other tools not listed above such as a vice which can be used instead of number 8, but you will see these as the tutorial progresses. 1 – Is 6mm cowhide lace from 1.8mm double shoulder veg-tanned tooling leather. 2 – Fiebings saddle soap. 3 – Dacron bow string waxed nylon thread. 4 – Artificial sinew. 5 – Fiebings Aussie conditioner. 6 – Tandy lace cutter (used to make the lace with). 7 – Craft knife with snap off blades. 8 – Weaver lace vice. 9 – Cut goat rawhide. 10 – Fall leather.

Alternative materials can be used for some of the above if you don't have them but the leather should be double shoulders of about 1.8 to 2mm thick or 4 to 5 oz – don't use kip; you need shoulders for the uniform thickness and density of that leather enabling you to use the whole hide. A **youtube** video shows how the use the lace cutter to make your own lace – it covers cutting from the middle but this tends not to make use of the whole. When I get the hide I trim around the outside as close to the edges as possible and then using the lace cutter, I lay the hide on my dining table (to take the weight and size of the hide) and cut my lace from the outer edge inwards – this way I can get the most quantity of lace from one hide, roughly 120 to 180m.

Apart from the leather you will need the Aussie conditioner, artificial sinew and strips of latigo or bridle leather for the falls (60cm by 10mm wide).

Day 1

Lace prep

Cutting lace method using 6 foot measurements as example

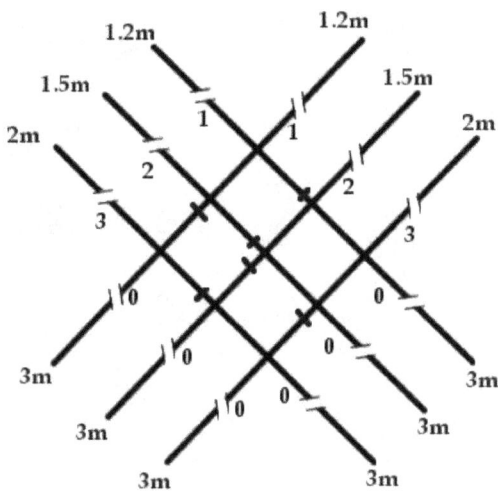

Length of each 12 laces;
1 = 1.2m
2 = 1.5m
3 = 2m
0 = 3m

| — middle of lace - measurements taken from here to the ends

0 — the tag number of each lace corresponding to its length

3m — length of each lace

These are doubled over and cut into
6 longer laces;

2 x 0 + 3 (5m x 2) = 10m — meaning to lengths of lace each 5m long are cut.
2 x 0 + 2 (4.5m x 2) = two lengths of 4.5m are cut
2 x 0 + 1 (4.2m x 2) = two lengths of 4.2m are cut

Many Whipmakers cut the lace they need to the lengths needed, i.e. for an 8 lace braid they would cut 8 lengths of lace and then attach each lace to the whip handle by sinew – I do not do this, for the 8 lace braid I cut 4 lengths of lace then half them, which means there are no loose ends one end of the whip. The photo below displays the typical lace length diagram I use to ascertain the different lengths of lace needed for any particular braid be it the 1st, core or 2nd inlay. So when I say 'Half' the lace, I mean one half maybe 1.5m long and the other half 3m long as shown above. Reason for this are to do with the gradual tapering of a whip where at various distances along the whip, laces have to be dropped.

Cutting lace

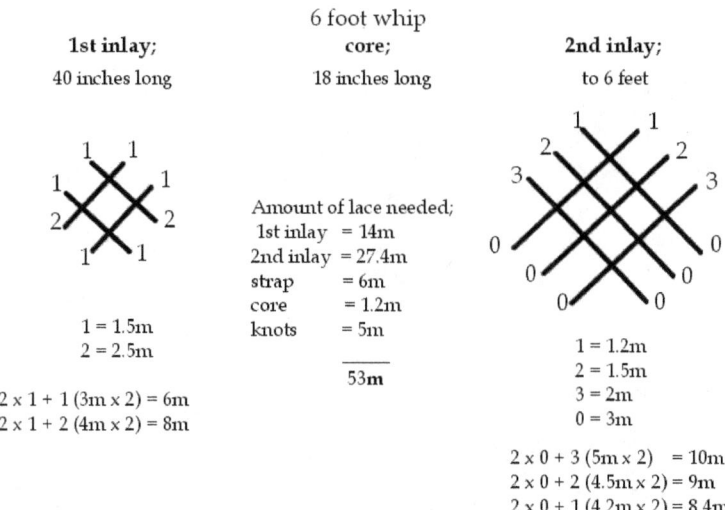

Lace prep of a whip may seem complicated and long winded, but it is necessary to achieve the tapered look of a bullwhip – The top photo displays the lace lengths needed and under each stage i.e. 1st inlay – 40 inches long, is stated the length of that stage needed. The bottom photo shows the cut lace set out in order of using them; 1 – is the 1.2m for the core, 2 – is the two lengths of 6m for 1st inlay. 3- Is the two lengths of 8m needed for the 1st inlay. 4 – Is the two lengths of 8.4m needed for the 2nd inlay. 5 – Is the two lengths of 9m needed for the 2nd inlay. 6 – Is the two lengths of 10m needed for the 2nd inlay. 7 – Is the 6m needed for the strap. 8 – Is the 1.5m needed for the transition knot. 9 – Is 3.5m needed for the top knot.

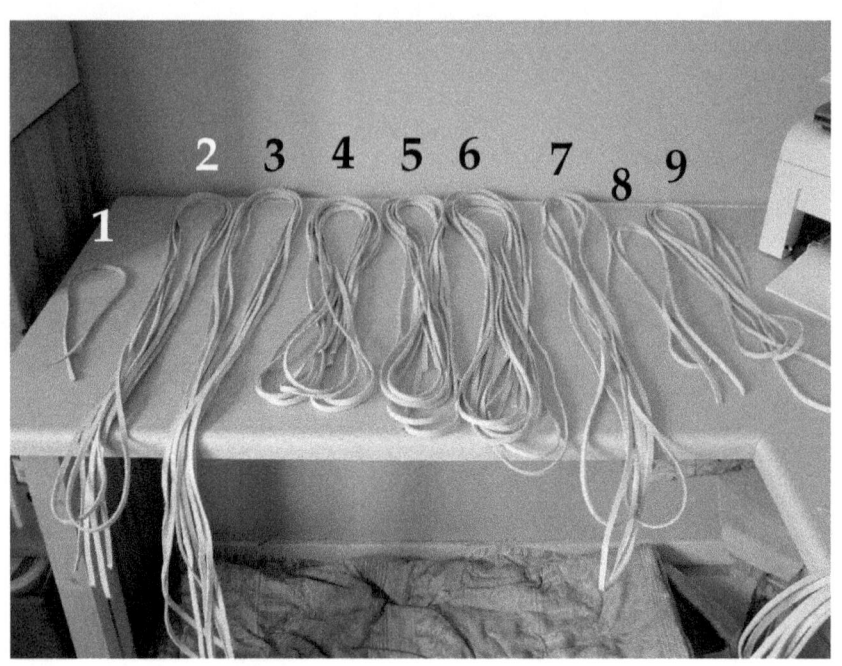

Bevelling lace

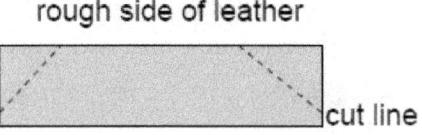

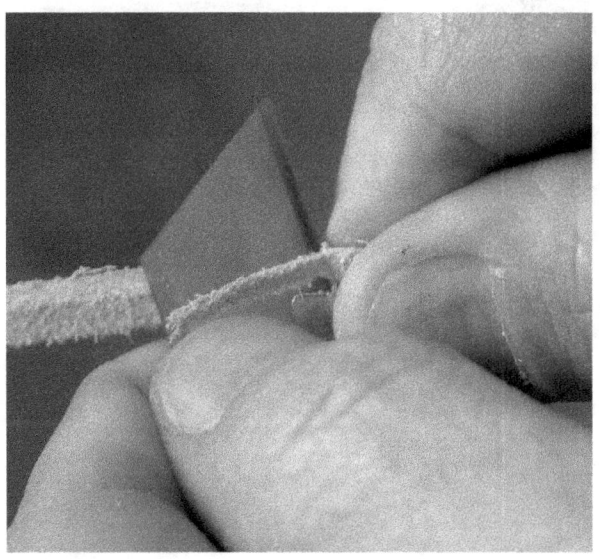

Next job is to bevel all the laces. Above, left displays the sort of angle and cut you are after, and above right shows my method of doing it. I attach one end into the weaver lace vice, then bevel backwards – there is an art to doing this and experience certaining makes it easier, the hardest part for a beginner is trying not to cut into the smooth side of the lace (and narrowing the wide of the lace) while trying to cut just the right amount of leather off – you probably will cut into the smooth side sometimes – just take your time and use a sharp knife, if the cut into the smooth side is to severe, you won't be able to use it for braiding.

Bevelling the lace this way also helps to stretch the lace and test it for weaknesses – its better if it breaks now then later while braiding.

Tapering laces

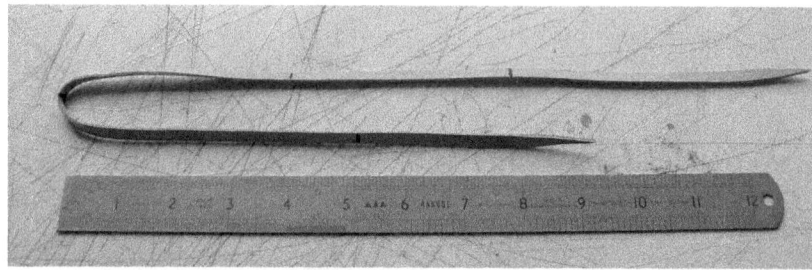

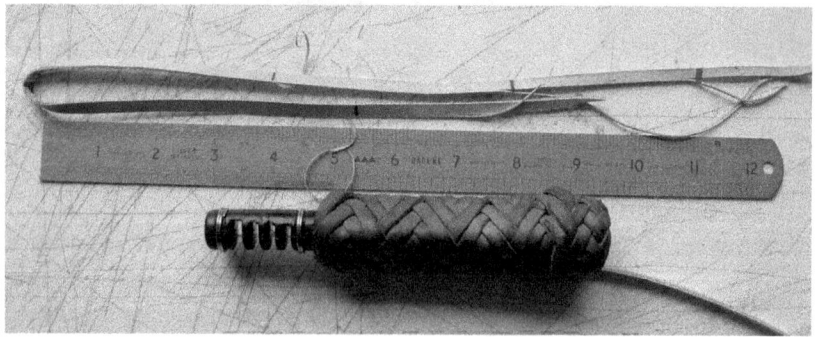

After bevelling, the core lace and those of the 1st inlay only have to be tapered. To start with find the middle of these laces and mark with a blue or black marker pen. Above is shown the core lace, it is the foundation from which the whip will be built on and is tapered as shown. Above top shows marks made as various lengths along the lace (distances are not important – staggering them is). Above bottom displays the lace after being cut (method shown below). Just trim off the lace and re-bevel on the sides of the lace which was tapered.

Above is displayed 2 lace cutters although one could be used. 1 - Provides the widest width lace and 5 the narrowest. The lace your using was cut at number 1 and I normally use 2 to 4 to taper my laces with – 5 is used for the loose core parts at the ends of the 1st and 2nd inlays.

The tapering of the 1st inlay is set out just like the core, starting with you making marks at various distances along the each lace, then using the widest cut first i.e. 2, taper the lace and re-bevel. The drawing on the next page displays examples of where and how often the laces are tapered.

1st inlay taper cuts

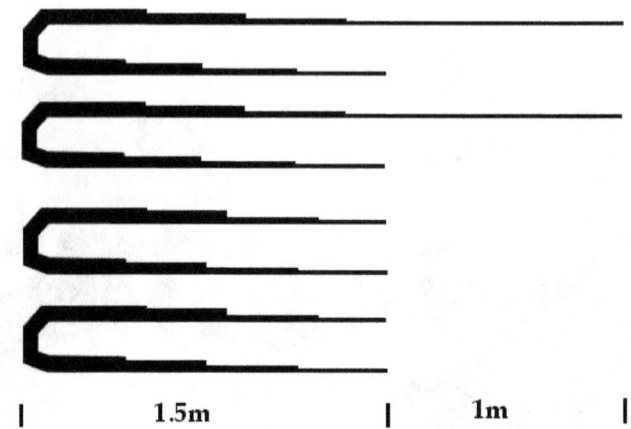

| 1.5m | 1m |

Dyeing and coating lace in Aussie conditioner

What you should have now is lace cut to length, all bevelled and the core and 1st inlays laces tapered. Next I set up my lace as shown in above left with the longer 1st and 2nd inlay laces draped over the back of the seat and the remainder laid out on the seat. Above right shows how I arrange dyes I am using plus shearling to apply dyes with, the Aussie conditioner, disposables gloves, all on top of a plastic bag. There is also plastic on the floor to stop any dye staining the floor and also to prevent the lace picking up any debris once the conditioner is on. All lace is dyed except for the core and 1st inlay – they are not seen and do not need it.

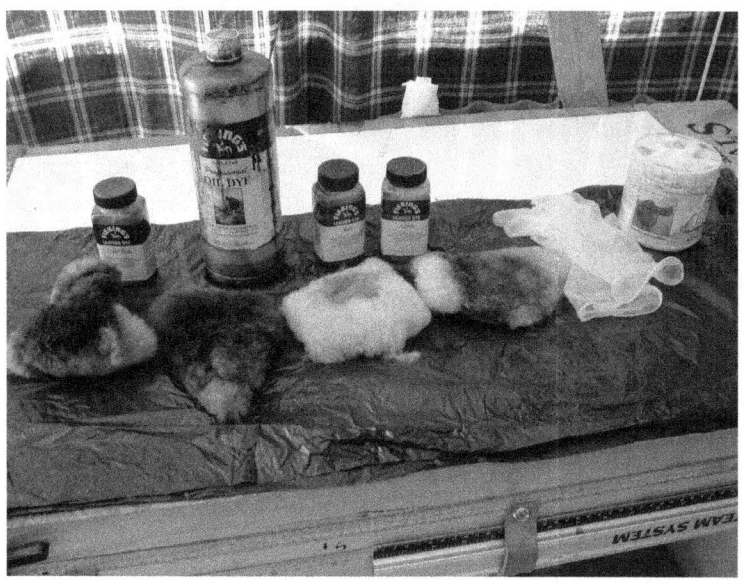

It is not important, nor necessary to have fancy dyed laces; for the Indy style whip all laces are just dyed a saddle tan colour, but dyeing the cowhide lace does seem to make it stiffer – I don't know if this means it's stronger but I have far less lace breakages from dyed lace as I do from undyed lace. The Photo above illustrates the importance of marking the centre or middle of the laces – To create some braided patterns as shown in the appendix, each side of a lace should be dyed different colours and having the centre marked helps locate where to start them and also aids when setting up the lace for braiding.

Now that the lace is dyed, coat all of them except for the core lace with a thin coat of Aussie conditioner – do this with the gloves you wore to apply the dye with. The conditioner is sticky and should be left on the lace to soak in overnight. The conditioner also stops the dye running.

Core and handle prep

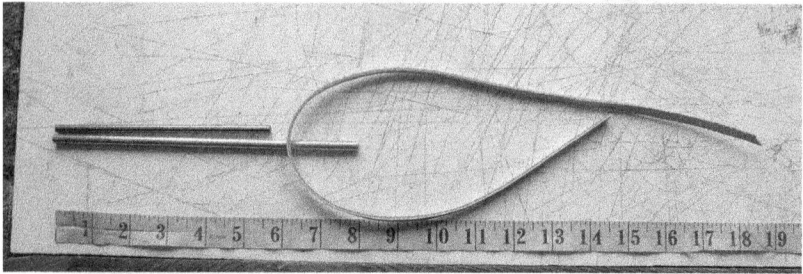

Materials I use to make up the handle are 6mm copper tubing with .5mm width that enables a 5mm steel rod to slide into it. As shown above the copper is cut to 8 inch and the steel rod to 5 – 6 inches, the ends of which should be filed to take away any sharp points. The tubing and steel rod are available from B & Q or similar hardware stores.

The difference in length between the steel rod and copper tubing is made up by the leather core, which after being twisted is pulled through the tubing and the steel rod pushed in behind it.

With the core leather bevelled and tapered, soak it under cold water, and then apply a generous amount of saddle soap along its length. Then follow above top ensuring that the smooth side rest against the nail – then twist the core leather together as shown above bottom – when you come to the ends bind the laces together with artificial sinew using the constrictor knot, as shown on next page. At the very end, tie the core around another nail – once it is firmly in place gently move the vice to pull the core tight, then coat in Aussie conditioner and leave in place for a few hours.

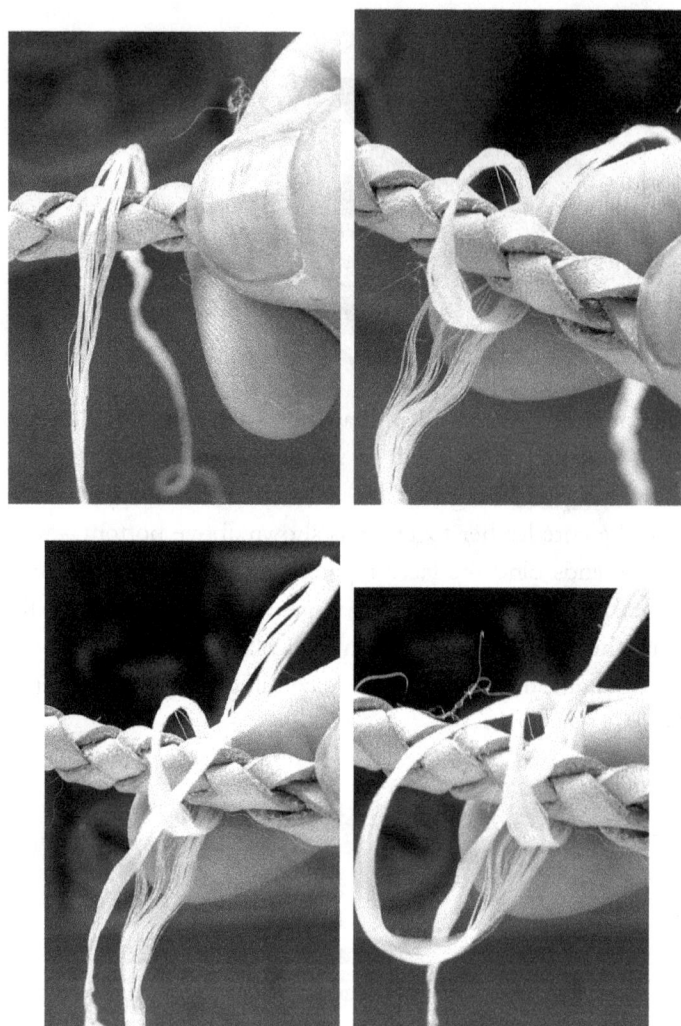

From left to right – drape sinew over braid, then fold each up to left and right leaving a slight loop. Next place right hand lace through loop, then lastly place left hand lace through and under loop and right hand lace – now tighten knot, cut and burn ends to fix in place. This knot is used extensively in the making of this whip

The first photo shows the leather core placed next to the tubing and rod. Above mid top shows the twisted core being pulled through a shorter piece of tubing – this helps round the core off and compress it slightly – ensure that the two laces are firmly tied together as they may try to unwind as you pull. Above mid lower show the core after it has been pulled through the copper tubing with the rod part way in – you will probably have to hammer it in lightly. Pulling the twisted core through the tubing helps round it further. Above bottom shows how I bind the transition between the leather and metal handle with artificial sinew – this helps to stiffen the junction slightly.

The knots I used for this tutorial are; for the transition, a 9 bight perfect pineapple knot and for the end, a 12 bight pineapple knot – instruction for these can be found in the appendix. They were built on a mandrel of 40mm diameter – nails for the 9 bight were spaced 55mm apart, for the 12 bight they were spaced 75mm apart.

Day 2

During this day you will be making the 1st **inlay** over the handle and core, then **bind** part way down it with artificial sinew which compresses the braid, strengthens the areas where lace was **dropped** – in a way it acts like leather bolster. After that the whip will be **rolled** to further compress and round up the thing, then your be able to make the end **strap** if you want one, make the **fall** which your need to before you start the 2nd inlay and lastly the **string**.

On the next page is a series of six photos taking you through the stages of starting a round 4 lace braid – The first photo has each lace numbered (corresponding to their lengths) to help you recognise where each belongs and also lettered, this will help you recognise where each lace is in relation to one another as you go through the braid sequence.

The sequence of this round braid is just like any other round braid, just has very few lace. The sequence is under 2 over 2 or u2, o2 for short. Notice how laces that start on the left or right, stay on the left and right as the braid progresses and that after the initial start, the topper most lace is the lead lace or the one that is braided next. This initial stage is braided loosely in the hand.

Braiding 1st inlay

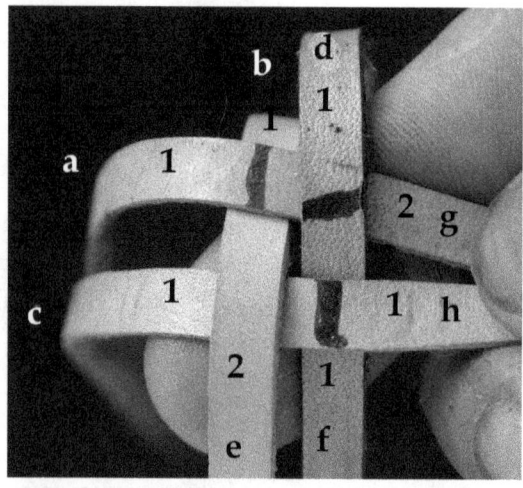

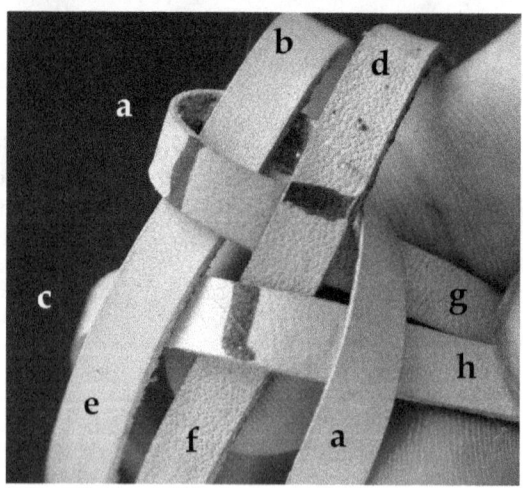

Figure 1 – this show how the lace should be held and positioned, Figure 2 – a, goes u2, o2

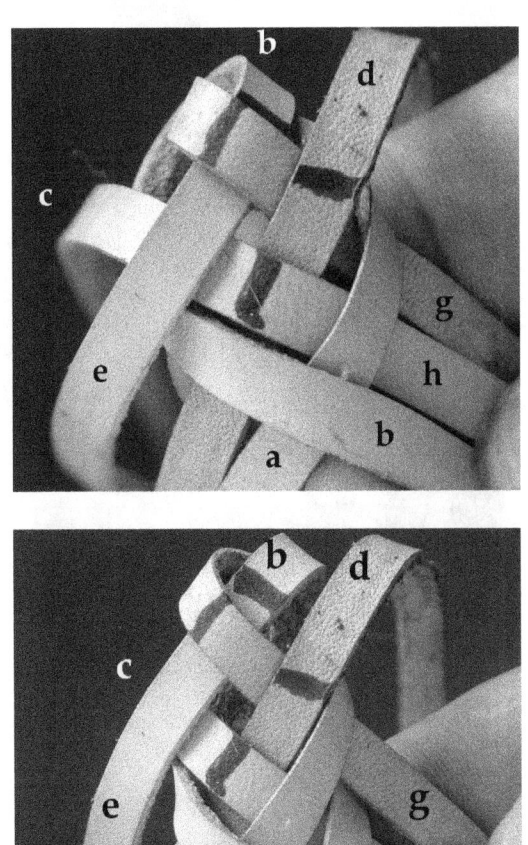

Figure 3 – b, goes, u2, o2, Figure 4 – c, goes u2, o2.

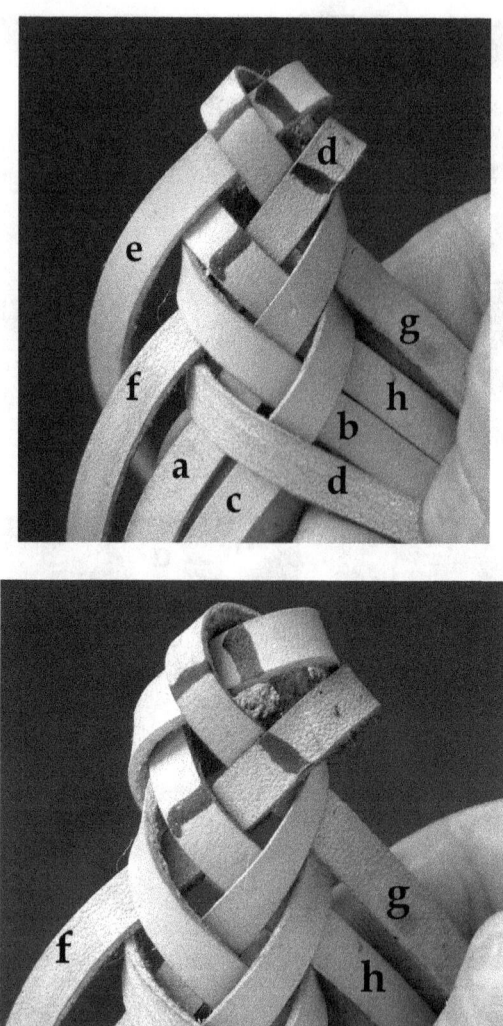

Figure 5 – d, goes u2, o2, Figure 6 – e, goes u2, o2

Photo 1 and 16a – After figure 6, the braid should be placed onto the end of the whip handle and each lace gently pulled until it looks similar to 16a – from here you continue the u2, o2 sequence starting with the topper most right hand lace marked as g.

Photo 2 and 17a – Braiding a whip thong differs to other braiding jobs, you need to pull and hold the lace tight in both hands with equal force – this is to ensure not only a tight compact braid but also that the braid runs evenly down the thong. In 17 you can see where I have been pulling more on the right then the right which has caused the braid pattern to twist slightly to the right. Photo 17a show how it should run. If this is your first whip, you will tend to pull more with your stronger hand – it is just a case of taking your time and concentrating on the force you exert with both hands.

Lace will break at some time or another, but it is not a total disaster. The method shown above can be used to extend the length of a lace as well as mend a break. First you need at least 5 inches of lace showing so start by unbraiding back until there is that amount of the broken lace exposed. Following the photo above from top to bottom, round off each end and skive the flesh side then using an old chisel the same width of the lace, cut a hole – open this out and thread each lace into the opposing hole – pull tight gently and flatten with a rubber hammer or other item, but gently. It is ideal if this mend can be hidden within one of the under moves of the braid sequence, and in most cases I find the 5 inches you left exposed, tends to be hidden but it is advisable to first test if where you make the hole on the broken lace will be hidden or not.

I tend to leave all the laces loose and untangle them after every braided move but some people like to wrap each lace into a bundle, as shown in above (not shown but in a bundle but string is normally wrapped around the middle) the loose end of lace shown under my thumb would be the lace your braiding with – remember to tighten the string every so often so that the bundle does not fall apart. Above right displays what I do if I have to leave the job – it is advisable to try and finish a run of braid but if you have to put the job down, tighten all the laces and then wrap them backwards around the vice or whatever item you're usi

Dropping lace on the 1st inlay is fairly straight forward, I used to drop them as done on the 2nd inlay but found it created to many bumps in the final whip – so now as shown above I just leave them loose, the braid they come out of and that of the binding will keep them in place and stop them loosening and as stated it creates a smoother taper. The reason why these laces were tapered was to ensure that the laces did not bunch up to much too soon and obviously help create the smooth flow of the tapering. But they will eventually start to bunch up as you progress down the core – as seen above and explained below. The sequence I use is to drop the short laces only is first on the left, then right, right and finally left, leaving 4 strings which are braided to 40 inches – this will leave the two longer strings which are twisted the same as the core laces were.

1st inlay - Dropping from 8 lace to 7 lace

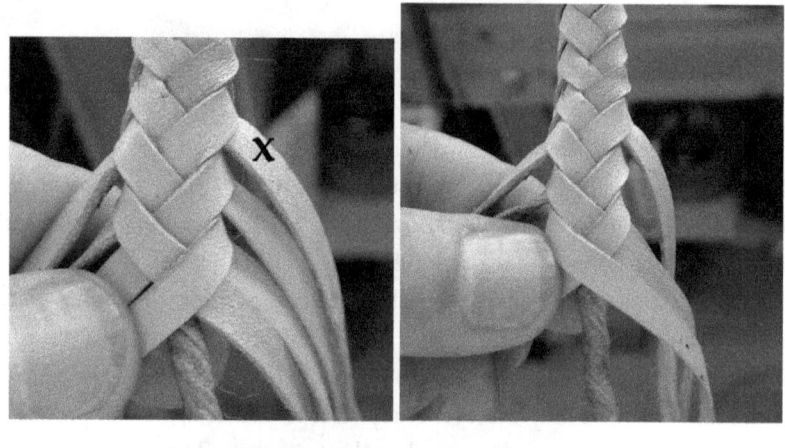

Photo 3, a,b,c – X marks the lace being dropped – sequence is braid the lace under X u2, o2, as shown in 21b, then braid from the topper lace on the left, u1 o2 as shown in 21c – from there on it is on the right side, u2,o2 and on the left side, u1,o2.

Dropping from 7 lace to 6 lace

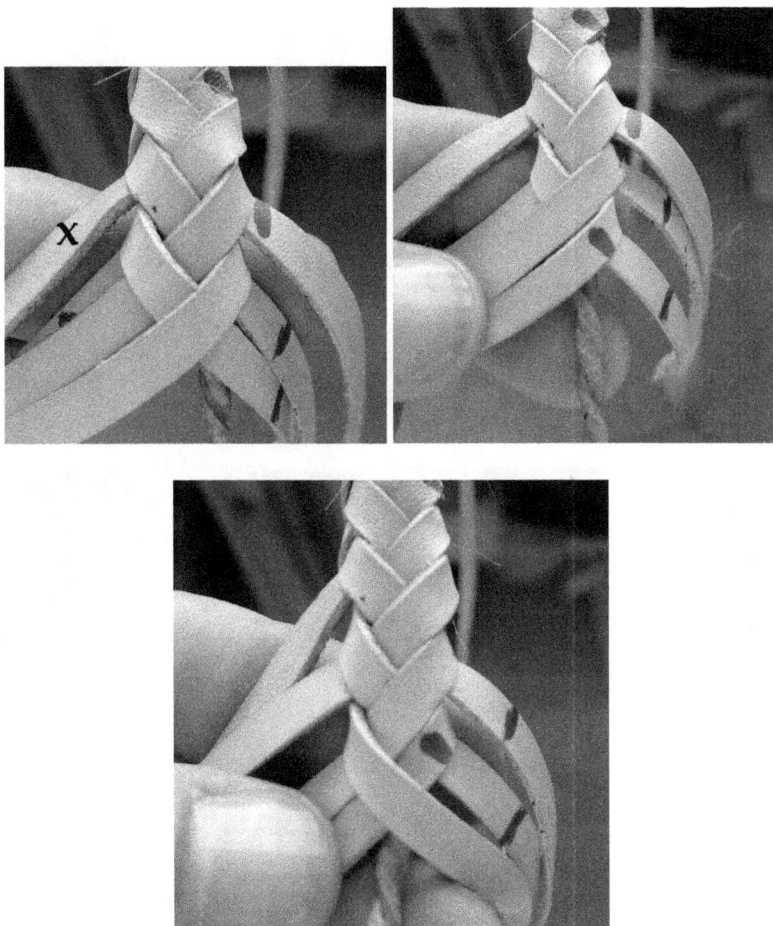

Photo 4, a,b,c – X marks the lace being dropped – sequence is braid lace under X u2,o1 as shown in 22b, then braid the topper lace on the right u1,o2 as shown in 22c. Sequence from here on is on the left side braid u2,o1 and on the right u2,o1.

Dropping from 6 to 5 lace

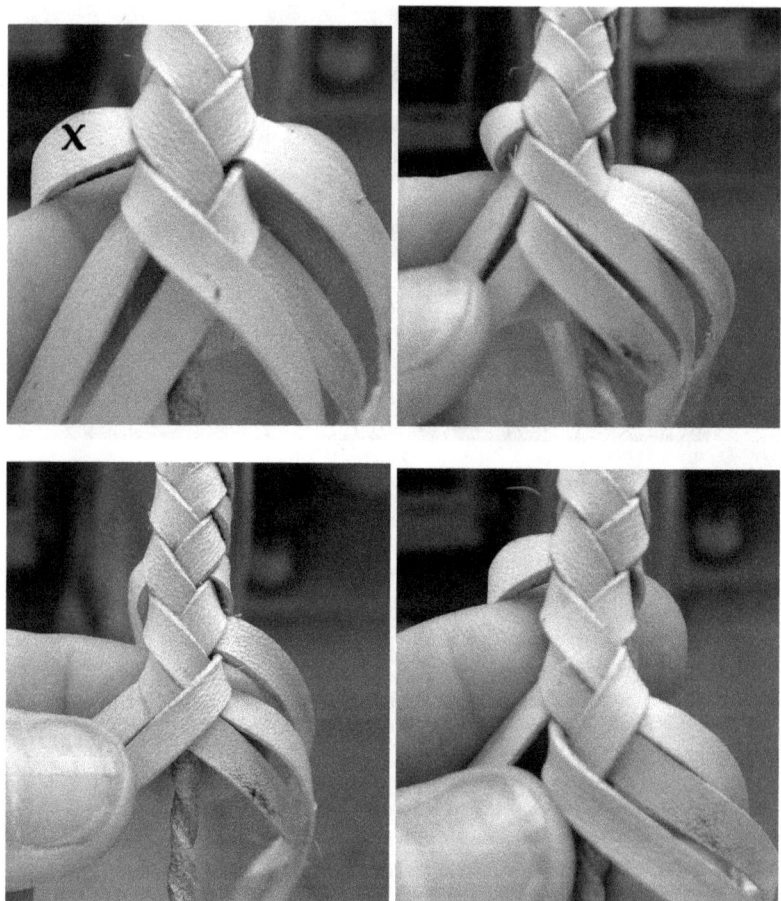

Photo 5, a,b,c,d – X marks the lace being dropped. Sequence is braid the top right lace u1,o1 as shown in 23b. Then braid middle left lace u1,o2 as shown in 23c. Next braid top left u1,o1 again as shown in 23d. Sequence from here on is from the left, u2,o1 and the right, u1,o1.

Dropping from 5 to 4 lace

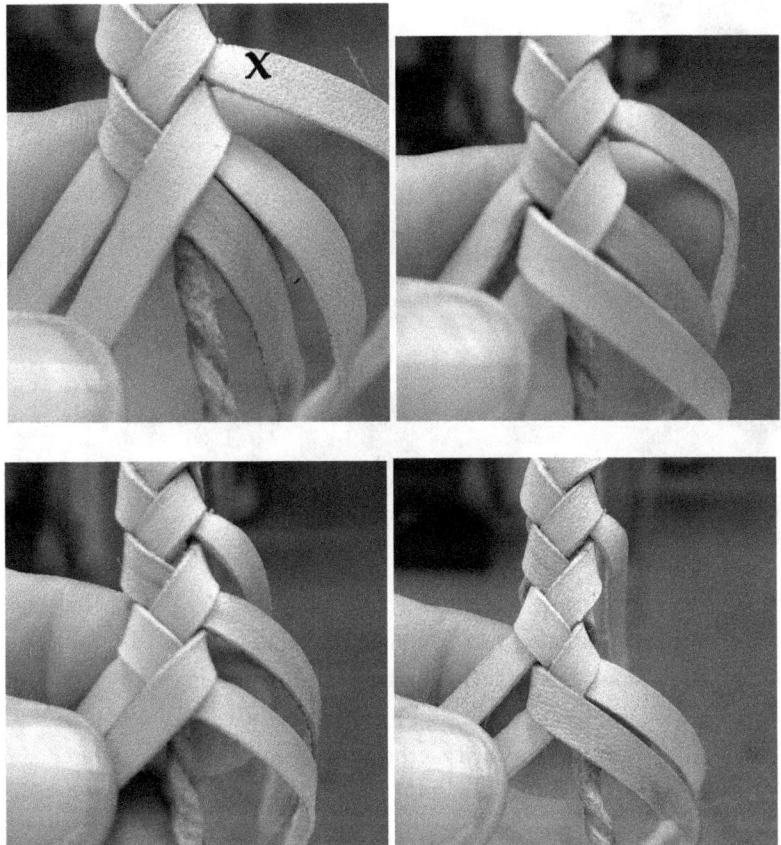

Photo 6, a,b,c,d – X marks the lace being dropped. Sequence is to braid the lace under X u1,o1 as shown in 24b. Then braid the top lace on the left side u1,o1 as shown in 24c. Photo 24d shows the top right lace braided u1,o1. Follow this sequence of u1,o1 for both sides until you reach 40 inches. When you have reached the 40 inches, tie off the 4 laces with constrictor knot.

Next you tighten the 4 laces you have dropped and cut them off as close to the thong as possible, then you need to roll the thong – I have a large 30mm thick slab of marble I bought from a stone mason/grave stone maker – I lay the thong on this and use a hard piece of wood to roll the thong backwards and forwards – the rolling really makes a difference in the look and feel of the braid.

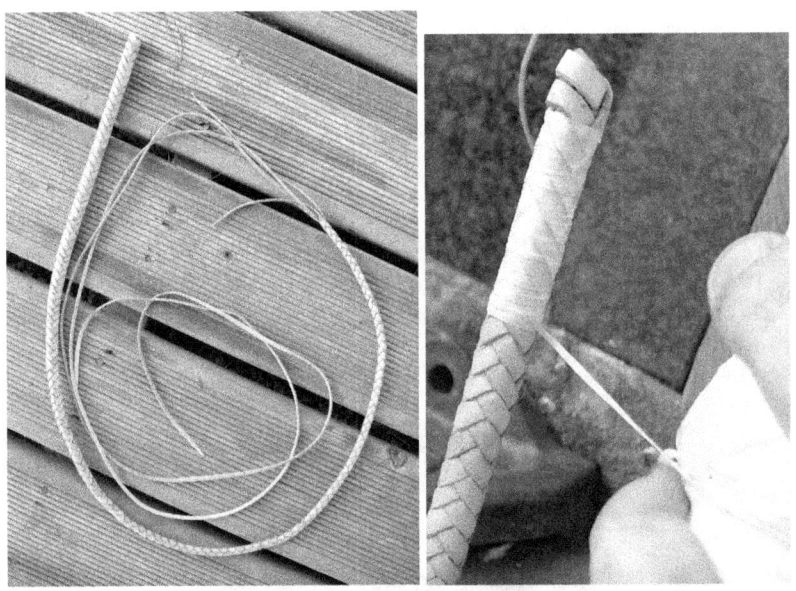

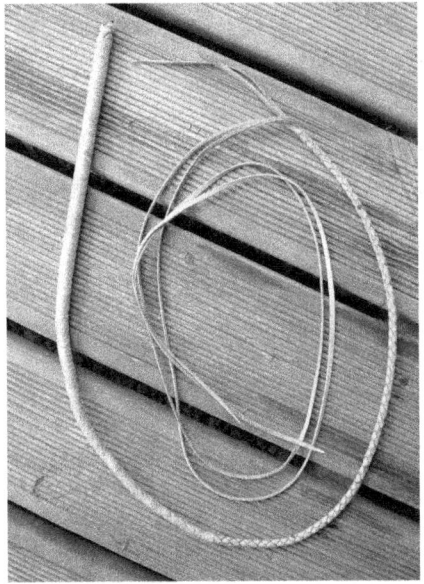

After this first rolling of the 1st inlay thong, your whip should look similar to top lef. Then place back into the vice to hold it firm while you wind the artificial sinew binder around the thong – start from the handle and progress down to just beyond where you dropped the last lace as shown in the bottom photo. Look in my 'Archers craft Book' to see how to tie off the end of the binding. After attaching the sinew, roll the thong again.

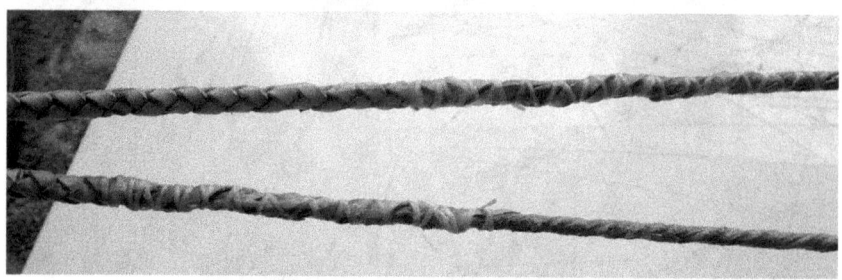

After rolling cut the remaining 4 laces to different lengths. Ideally the two short ones to 2 and 6 inch and the two longer ones to 15 inch from where you tied them all off – the last one you cut to 6feet from the handle end of the thong. Next using the 5th cutting size of the lace cutter as shown on page 14, narrow the two longer laces and re-bevel (narrow each to just before the ends of previous laces). Place the ends of the thong in the vice again – wet the 4 laces, coat in saddle soap and twist together and tie off each lace against the core and make the end firm with a nail. To make the junction from braid to twisted laces stronger wrap artificial sinew around the transition area from just beyond the braid to where the second lace was cut as shown in the top photo – this helps to strengthen this area and not make it too floppy. When done pull the vice back slightly to make the core taut and leave for a few hours then take out and re-roll the whole thong including the extended core.

1st inlay and extended core after being rolled.

8 lace end strap

The braid explained below allows for a variety of patterns to be created depending on the colours and how you dye the 8 strands, this photo just shows two variations. The next photo shows how I anchor the strap after I have hand braided about 8 inches of it – it is the same method I use for braiding belts etc. The hardest part of doing a flat braid is keeping it all even, and just like with the lace for the whip thong you have to get accustomed to pulling the lace equally on both sides. Before starting you need to divide the lace for the strap into 4 lengths, then find the half way points of each and start as below.

Figure 1, 2, 3 – 1- lay the lace as illustrated. 2- Back braid the top left lace o1, u2. 3 – Back braid the top right lace o1, u1.

Figures 4, 5, 6 – 4 – back braid the top right lace o1. 5- Back braid the last right hand lace back on its self o2, u1. 6 – Back braid the top right lace u2, o1.

Figures 7, 8, 9 – 7- back braid the top left lace o2, u2. 8 – Back braid top right hand lace o2, u1. 9 – Back braid top left lace u2, o2.

Figure 10, 11, 12 – 10 – braid top right lace u2, o1. 11 – Braid top left lace u2, o2. 12 – Shows the braid you have done already tightened up. The sequence from here is to braid to 4 repeating moves– braid sequence now is; R_1 – o2, u1. L_1 – u2, o2. R_2 – u2, o1. L_2 – o2, u2 – repeat from R_1.

47

Carry on braiding until your strap is similar in length then that shown in the top photo, ensuring you can get your hand through the loop. Once you have enough braided, tie off the end by wrapping it with electrical tape – lightly hammer and cut off ends.

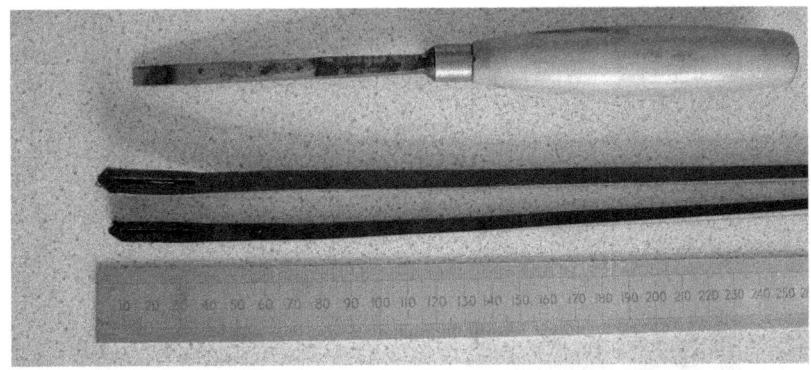

These two photo display the length (60cm) and width of the fall (6 – 10mm tapering to 0mm). After they are cut, make a hole in the wider end as shown plus use a grade 1 edger to smooth the edges. That's the fall done. The traditional material used is white hide, if you can get it use it, other wise use latigo or bridle leather – needs to be thick and dense.

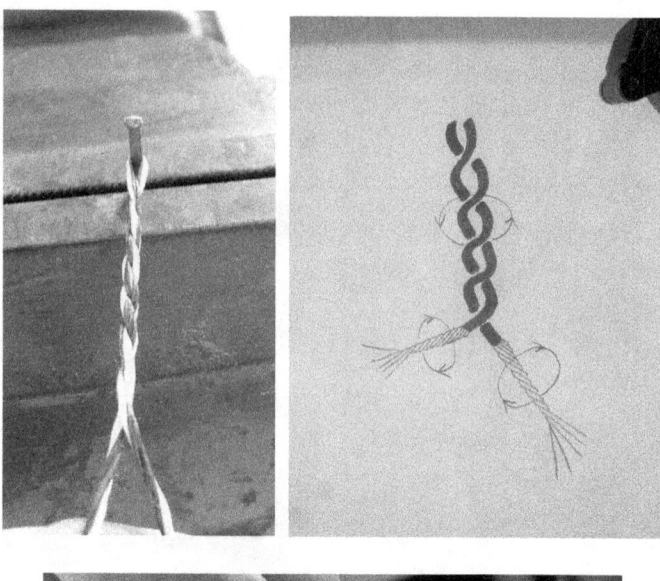

For my strings I use dacron, I cut 6 lengths of 85cm long, double these over and twist as shown in above. Top right shows how to twist. Near the end I take the left hand bundle of strings, make a loop and thread then around the loop twice than pull tight, as shown in the bottom photo. Cut off the ends to within 1 inch of the knot and that's the string done.

Day 3

Today I cover the 2nd and final inlay braid, which leads onto fixing on the fall, the string and then a whole lot of fun rolling, rolling and rolling the whip. After that it will just be a case of fixing on the transition and top knots along with the strap. Then finally after all your hard work your be able to go outside and test it.

The instructions for the 2nd inlay will begin with starting the braid, and then go onto the handle braid which in this case is based on a braid called 'the bird's eye' from Ron Edwards making whips book. Then lastly I will cover the dropping laces along the thong.

The start braid is pretty much the same as it was for the 1st inlay but with more laces to handle – can be difficult but if you follow the photos you should be OK – make sure that the middle/half way point of every lace is marked and that you have them lined up in order of shorter laces to longer laces – the photo above displays how I arranged the 1st inlay laces with all the longer lengths facing the furthest from me and the shortest, nearest to me. When you have the laces arranged as in fig 1 below check that all the shorter laces are facing away from you, the longer one's towards you.

Starting 2nd inlay braid

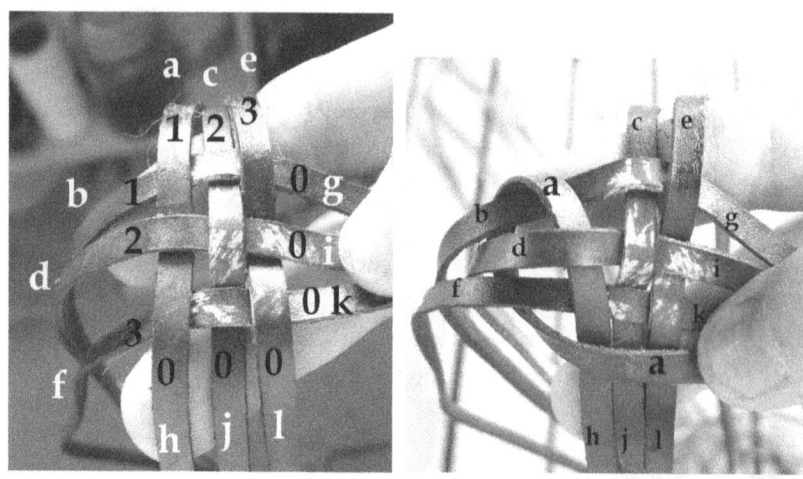

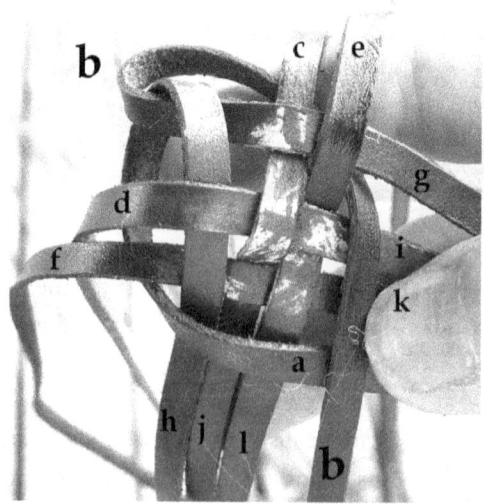

Figure 1 – lace positioned as shown in photo 4, fig2 - move a u3, o3, Fig3 – b u3, o3.

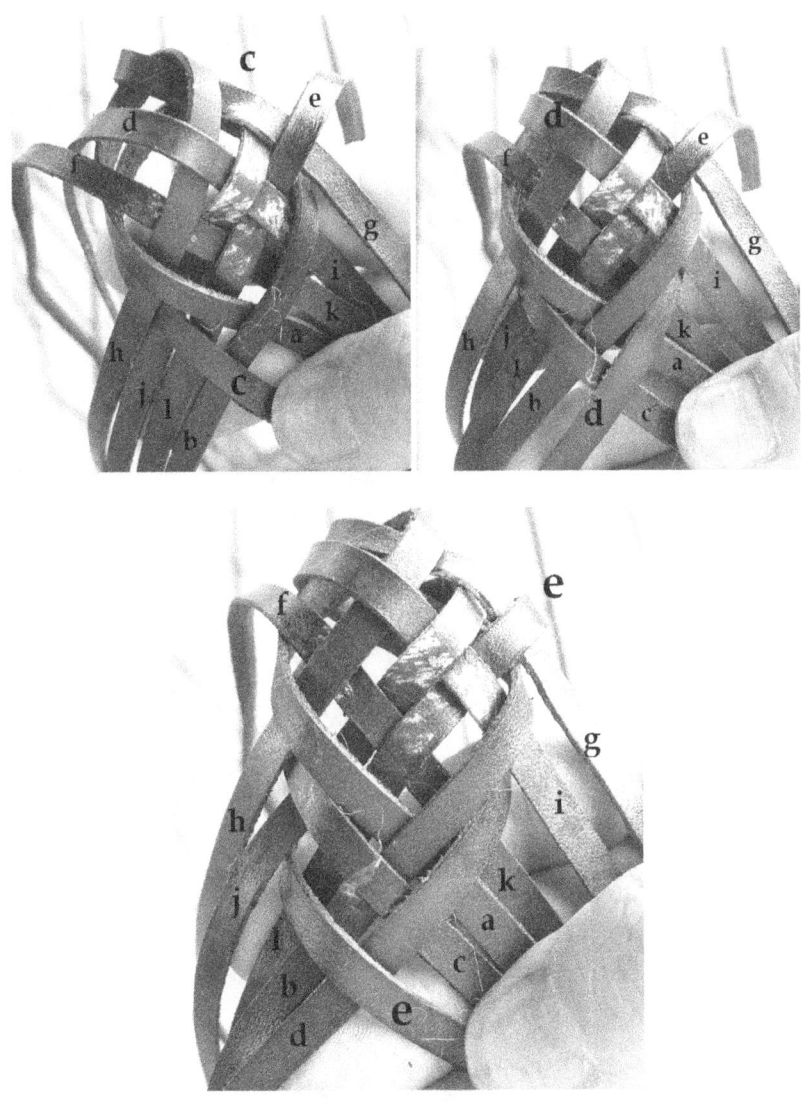

Figure 4 – c u3, o3, Fig 5 – d u3, o3, Fig 6 – e u3, o3

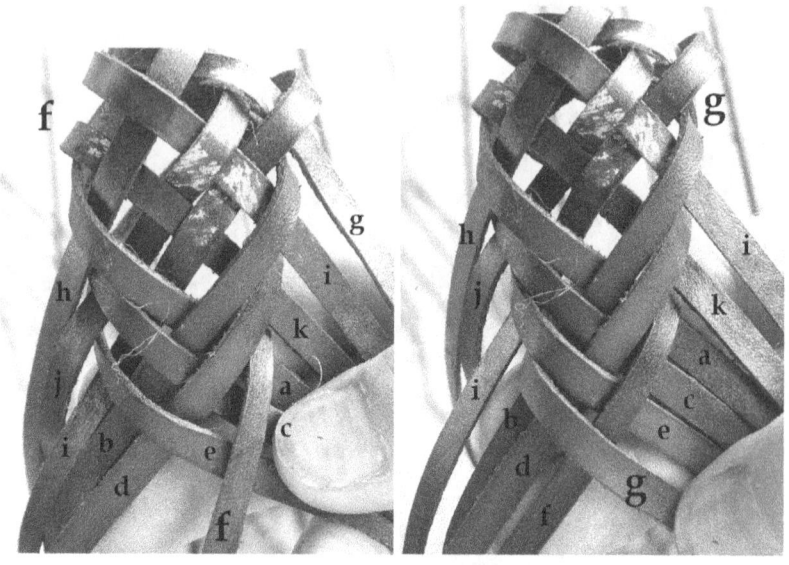
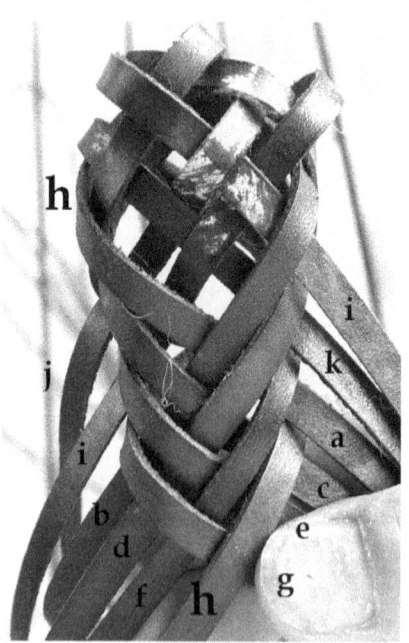

Figure 7 – f u3, o3, Fig 8 – g u3, o3, Fig 9 – h u3, o3

Once you are as far as Fig 9, slide the braid onto the end of the handle and tighten all laces as shown. If you have dyed the laces different colours, ensure that you pull equally on both ends of it to ensure that the half way mark stays near the top. After tightening like above slide back over end of handle and tighten the laces again to hide the laces of the 1st inlay.

Handles braid

Handles of whips can be braided in many different fashions, if you wanted more of a Indy style looking whip, then from the start braid you would braid in a sequence of u2, o2 u2 starting with the top right hand lace in this instance. I like to use the bird's eye braid because I prefer it but the Indy style is an easier alternative if you prefer that. At the point of transition or where the metal handle ends and the leather thong begins – the changing from the Indy style to the thong braid is much the same as I describe for the birds eye i.e. from a sequence of u2, o2, u2 you just start u3, o3 with the topper most lace. All the areas where braided patterns change will be hidden later by the knots.

The sequence of the birds eye differs to those already covered, as in you braid two lace on one side at a time i.e. - 1R , u3 o3 – 2R, u2 o2 u2 followed by 1L, u3 o3 – 2L, u3 o3. All will become clear below.

It is important that you braid the laces in order and follow a sequence, if you fail to do this it will mix up the lengths of the laces and make dropping of them difficult – if this happens you just have to back braid to where the problem started.

You will see that I have braided a length of the bird's eye already – this is more so you can see what it looks like. This braid tends to harder to keep tight, so as well as keeping the lace tight while braiding, I normally tighten all the laces after a run of 4 moves.

The two blue marks are there to help me tell where to change from the handle braid pattern to the thong pattern. The bottom mark indicates where the thong starts bending; the top mark indicates where I start changing the braided pattern.

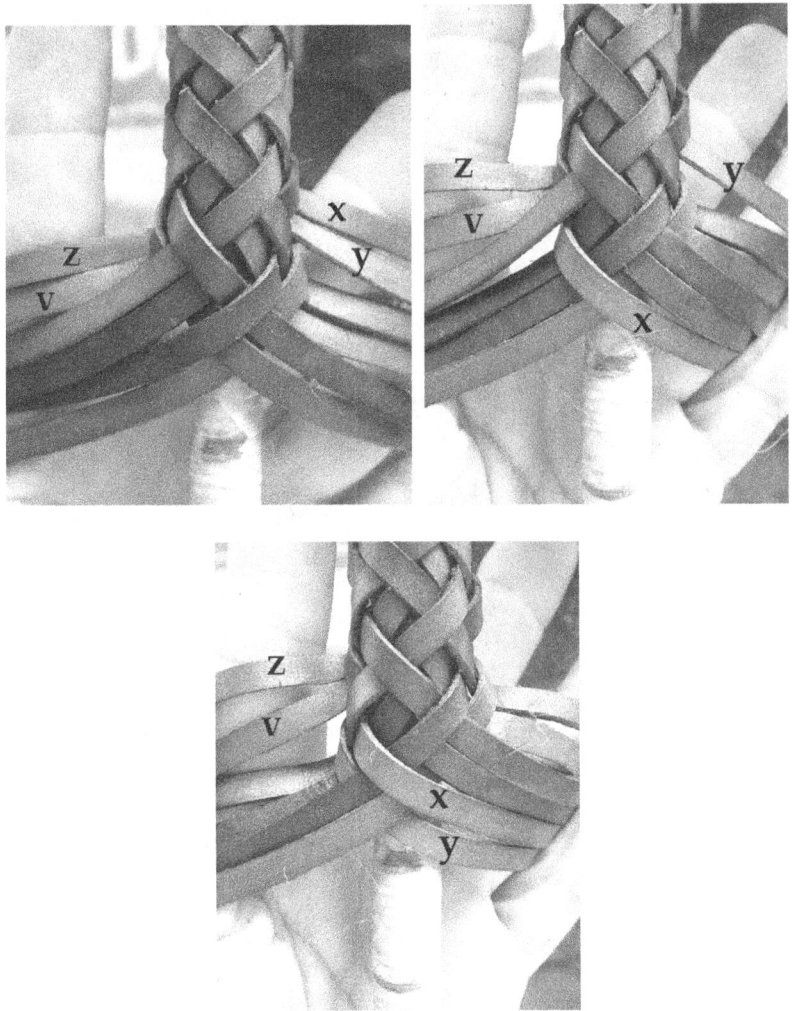

Figure 1 – Following on from the start braid, your top lead lace (fig 9 lace i) should be on the right, marked as X in fig 1 above. Fig 2 – Braid X back under 3 and then forward over three. Fig 3 – Braid Y back under 2, then over 2 and finally under 2 to end up resting underneath X.

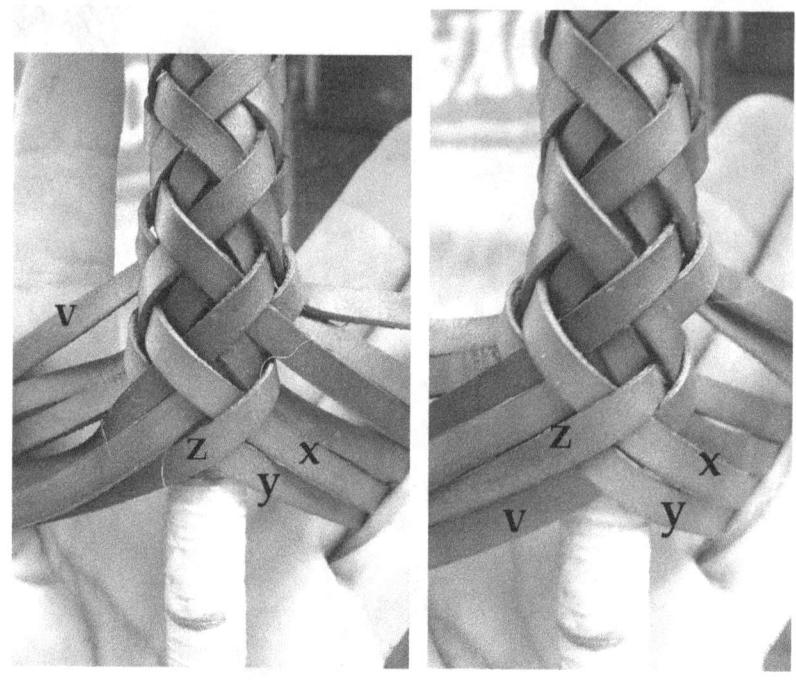

Now working with the left hand laces, braid Z under 3, over 3. Fig 5 – lastly braid V under 2, over 2, under 2. Carry on this sequence till the top blue mark is reached – push up the braid slightly and tighten all the lace, then follow the sequence below to start the u3, o3 sequence of the leather thong.

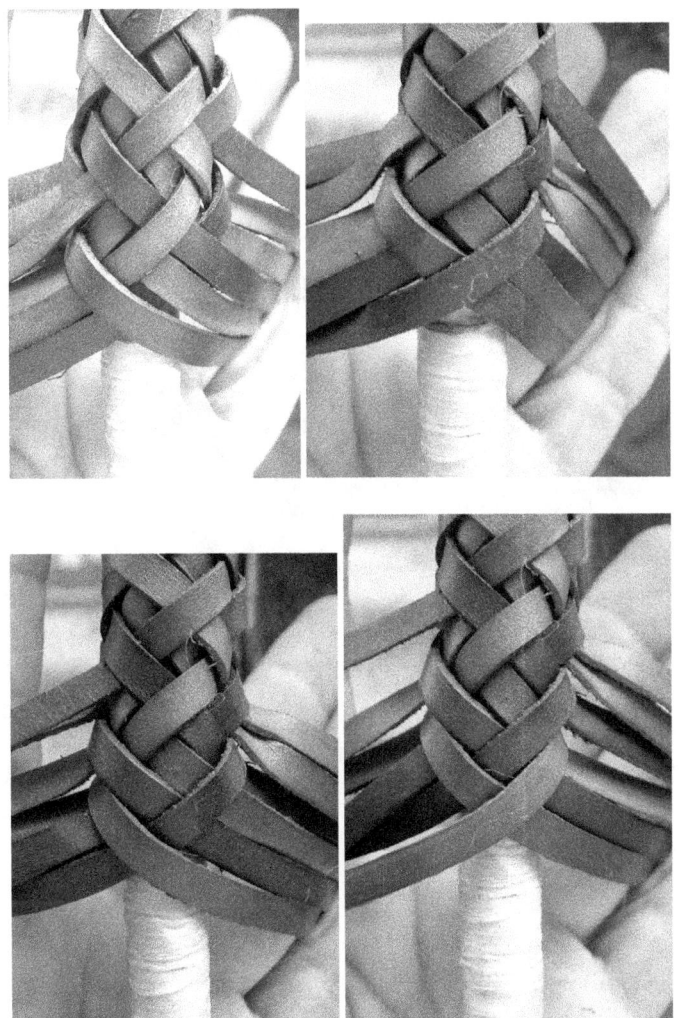

As shown above, you now stop the u2, o2, u2 sequence of the bird's eye and just carry on with the u3, o3 also reverting back to braiding one lace on a side at a time.

Cutting dropped laces

When you come to drop laces the above will make more sense – the lace of the 2nd inlay were not tapered so will bunch up more as can be seen in the photo's above along the thong – when you come to drop these lace's , you are dropping two at a time and need to be hidden from view – this is done by first skiving the lace as shown above left (to prevent too much bulge) and then the lace is narrowed as shown above right (again to reduce the bulge created) – I normally do these two while the whip is still in the vice, but as a beginner it may help to rest the whip on a table. Done my way, I gauge when best to drop the laces, and then carry on braiding until the two shortest laces on both side are positioned at the bottom – tighten all the laces and tie off all those I do not need. Then using the craft knife skive the leather then narrow.

Some might find skiving with a craft knife to awkward, another cheap alternative is shown above – converting a lace cutter into a sort of skiver – All I did was remove the blade and using a chisel, cut away the plastic between the last two holes, filed it slightly and glued onto the cutter part of another blade – I have used this to help skive the laces to be dropped but had to do it with the whip out of the vice – the ends of the laces to be skived will need to be skived in order for them to fit into under the blade.

Dropping 12 to 10 laces

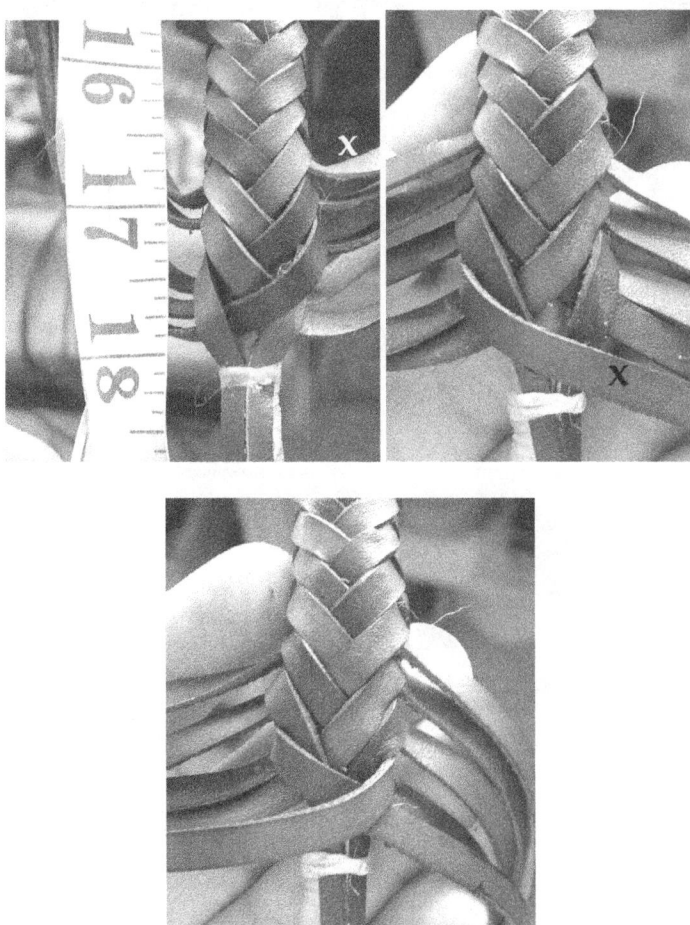

Shown here is the skived and cut lace tied to the core loosely with a constrictor knot, loosely as you will need to be able to pull them. The tape is measured from the top of the whip and gives a guide as to when the laces should be dropped on this whip. X marks the top lead lace which will be braided first. Fig 2 – X has been braided under 3, under 2. Fig 3 – lead lace on left side has been braided under 3, over 2.

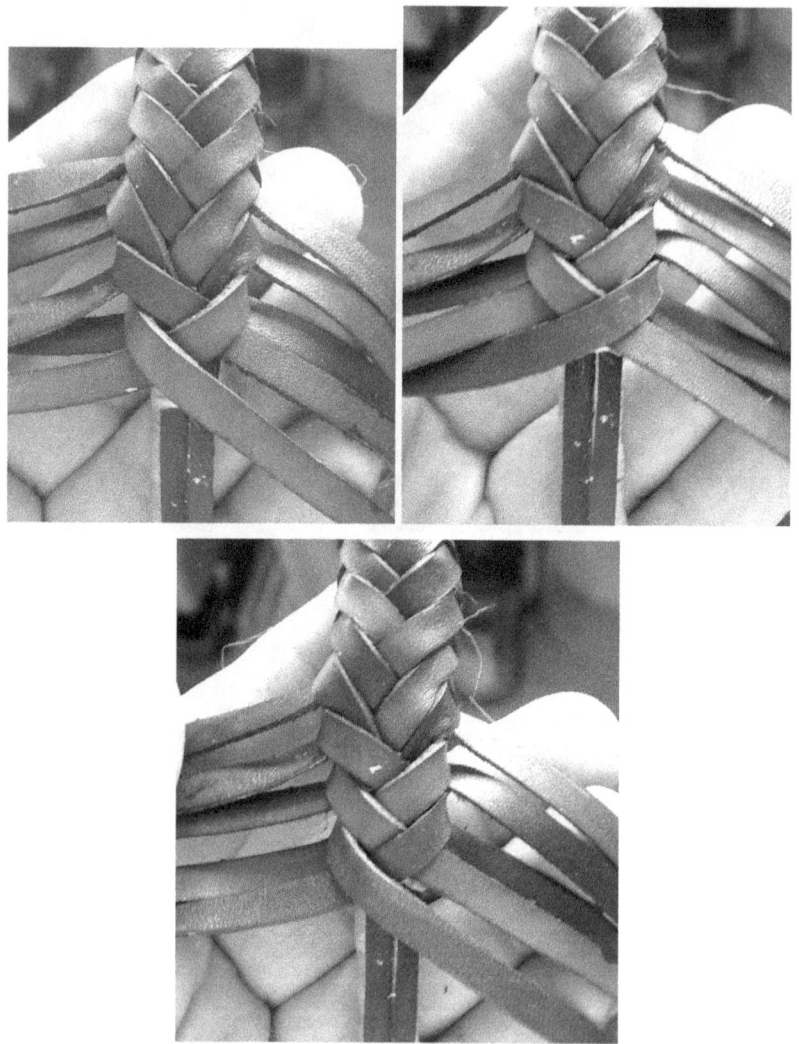

Figure 4 – top right lace is braided u3, o2. Fig 5 – top left lace braided u3, o2. Fig 6 – top right lace braided u3, o2. From this point tighten all the laces including the dropped laces, then cut them off just below the last braided lace – carry on braiding u3, o2.

Dropping 10 to 8 lace

Figure 1 – displays distance that these laces were dropped. Fig 2 – top right lace braided u2, o2, notice how this lace rest just under the blue lace. Fig 3 – top left braided u2, o2, notice again how this lace is placed just under to tan lace. Fig 4 – braid top right u2, o2.

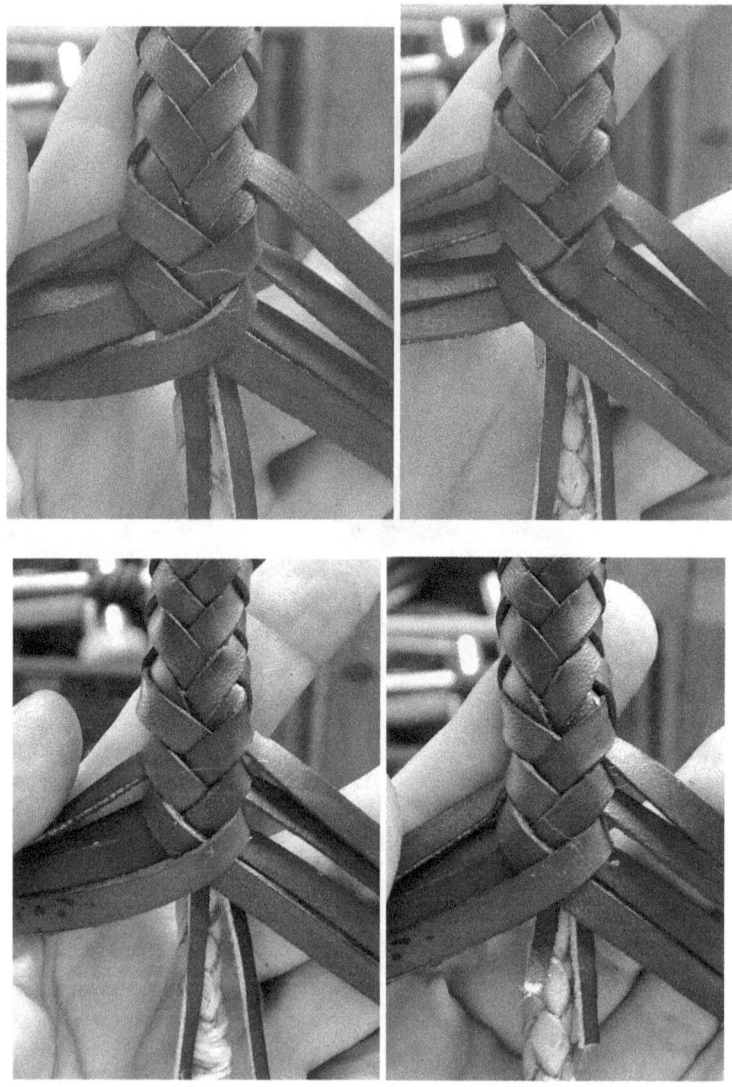

Figure 5 – top left u2, o2. Fig 6 – top right u2, o2. Fig 7 – top left u2, o2. Fig 8 – tighten all the laces including the two dropped ones and cut off – then continue braiding u2, o2.

Dropping from 8 to 6 laces

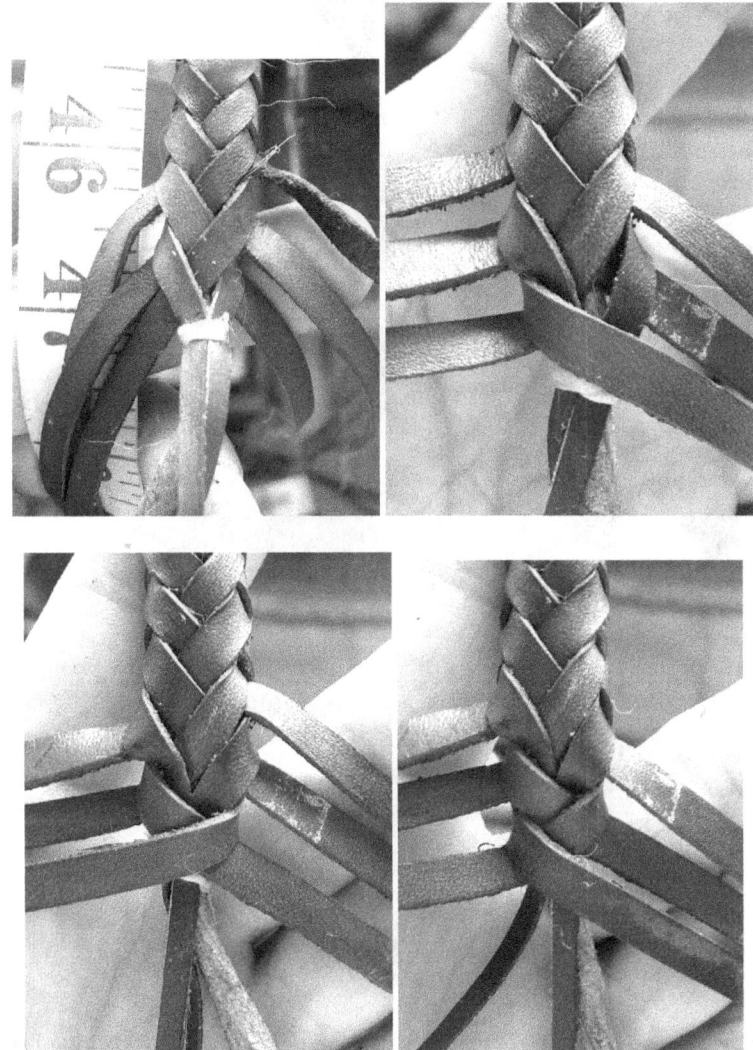

Figure 1 – shows distance from top of whip. Fig 2 – top right lace braided u2, o1. Fig 3 – top left lace braided u2, o1. Fig 4 – top right lace u2, o1.

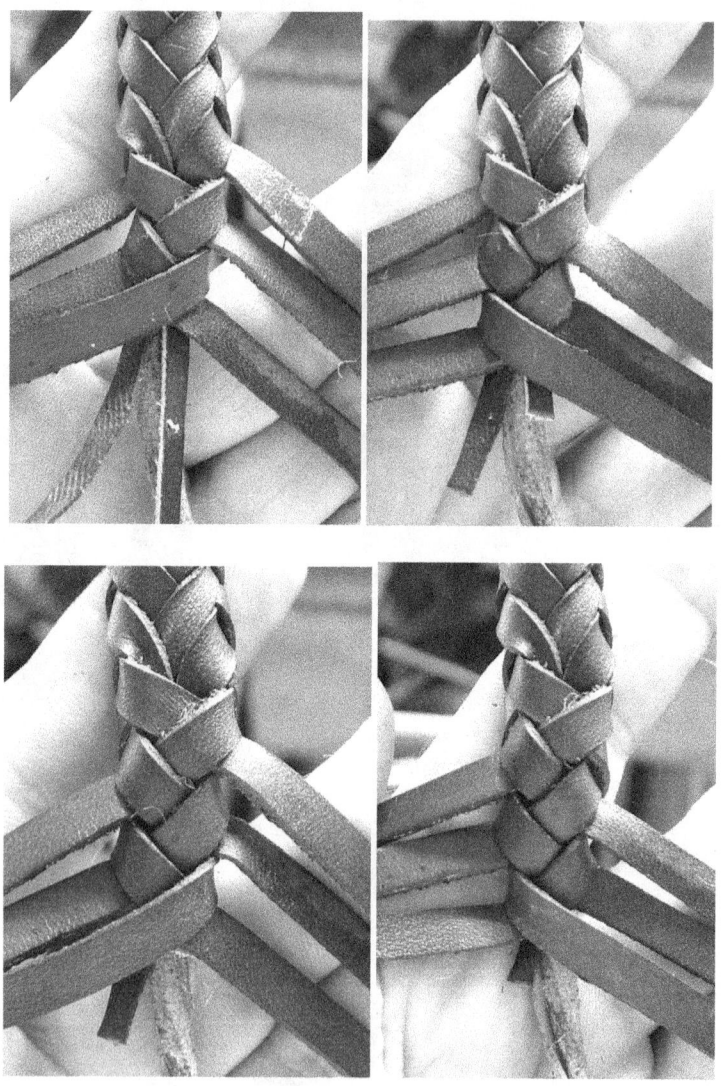

Figure 5 – top left u2, o1. Figs 6 – tighten all laces and cut dropped lace, then braid top right u2, o1. Fig 7 – top left u2, o1. Fig 8 – top right u2, o1. Carry on braiding u2, o1 till end of core or follow next drop if wanted.

Dropping lace 6 to 4

I don't normally drop below 6 laces but have included it in case anybody wants to try it. It does create a narrower thong but normally creates a weak joint.

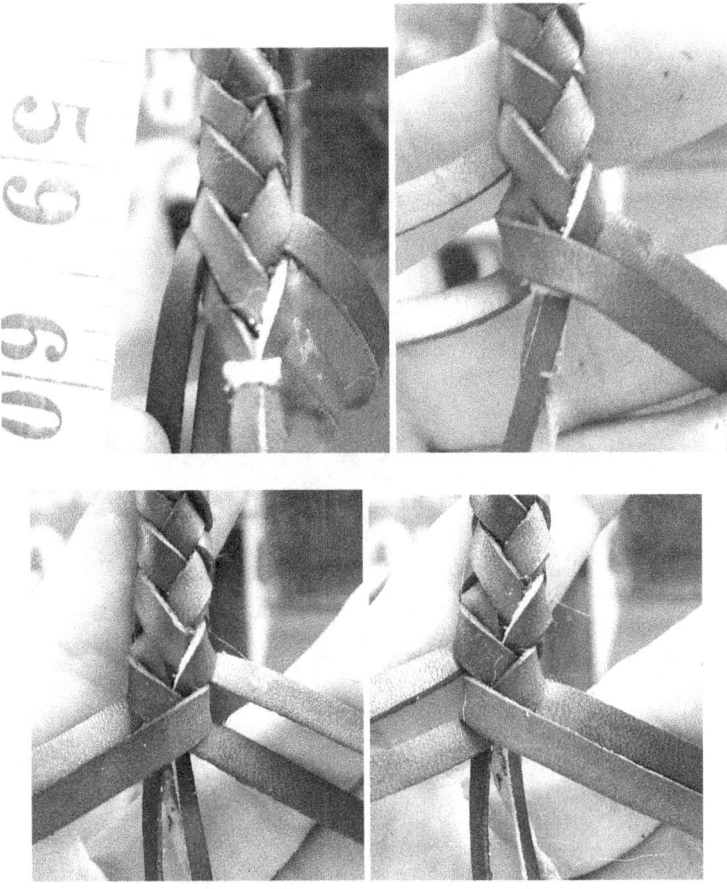

Figure 1 – Distance from top of whip. Fig 2 – top right lace u1, o1 (as with 10 to 8 drop, lace should rest under top one). Fig 3 – top left lace u1, o1. Fig 4 – top right u1, o1 tighten all laces and cut dropped ones.

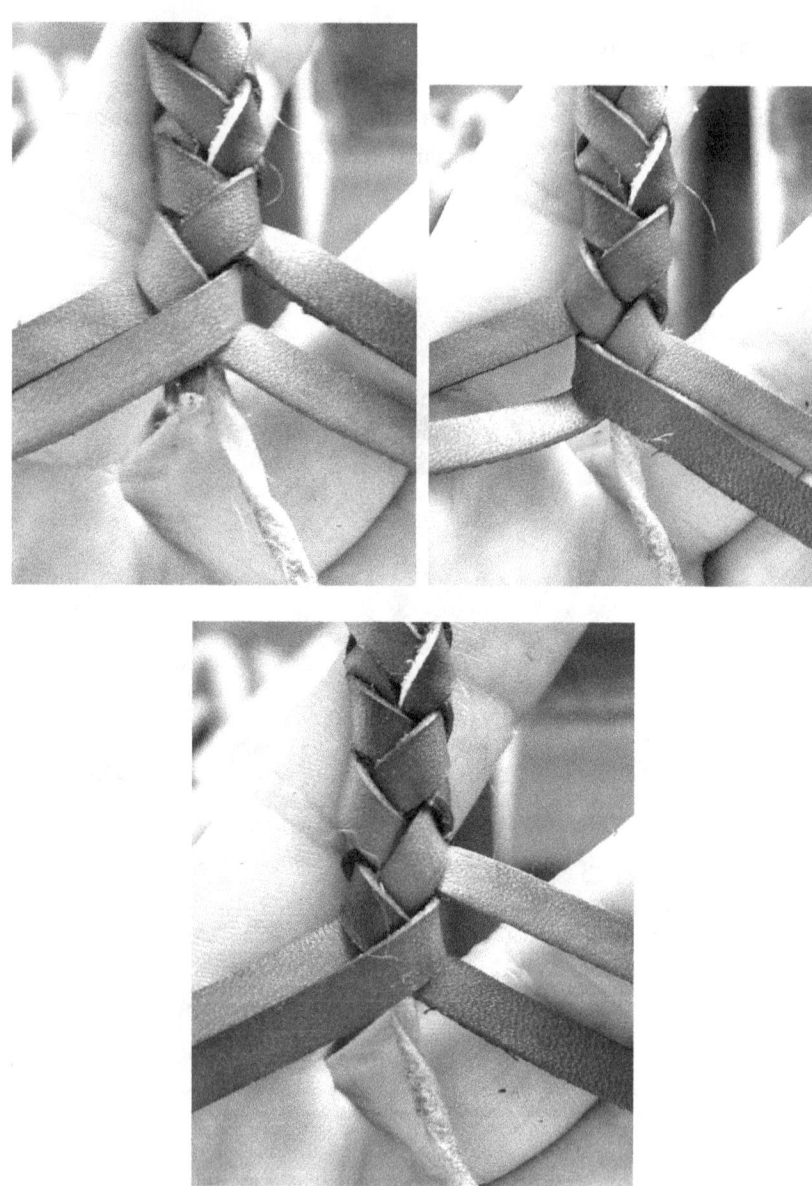

Figure 5 – top left lace u1, o1. Fig 6 – Top right u1, o1. Fig 7 – top left u1, o1. Carry on braiding u1, o1 till end of core.

Fixing on fall

In all the many whips I have made, I have never been able to achieve the neat, pretty little knots that the pro's, instead I finally rested on the knot below – it may not be the prettiest in the whip world but it does the job.

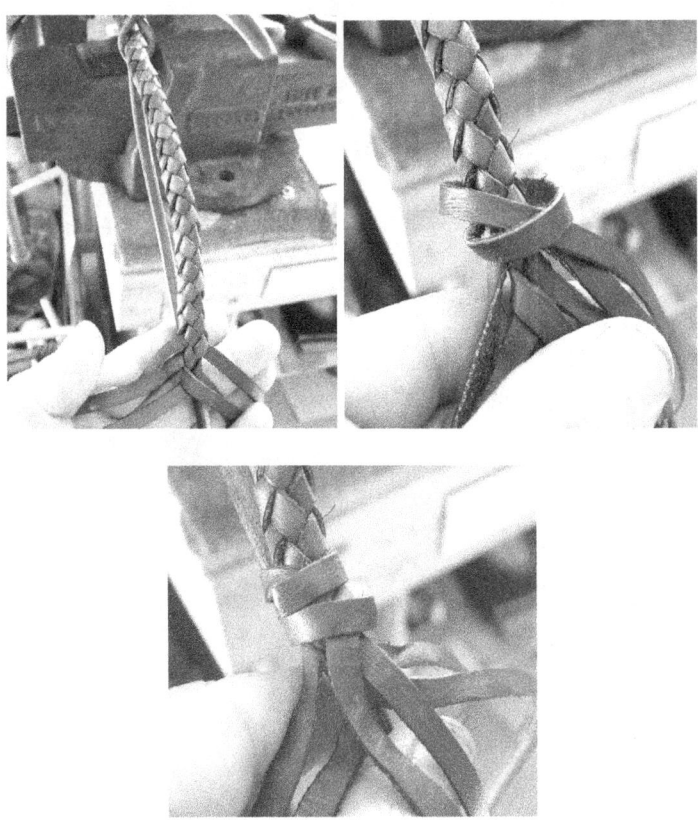

Figure1 – First I place the end of the thong through the hole in the fall and pull it up a distance – I do this to take advantage of the taper in the fall, which as it is pulled down should tighten the knots made even more. Fig 2 – use the top left lace and wind it left around the thong and fall and thread through the loop made – tighten. Fig 3 – do the opposite with the top right lace – tighten.

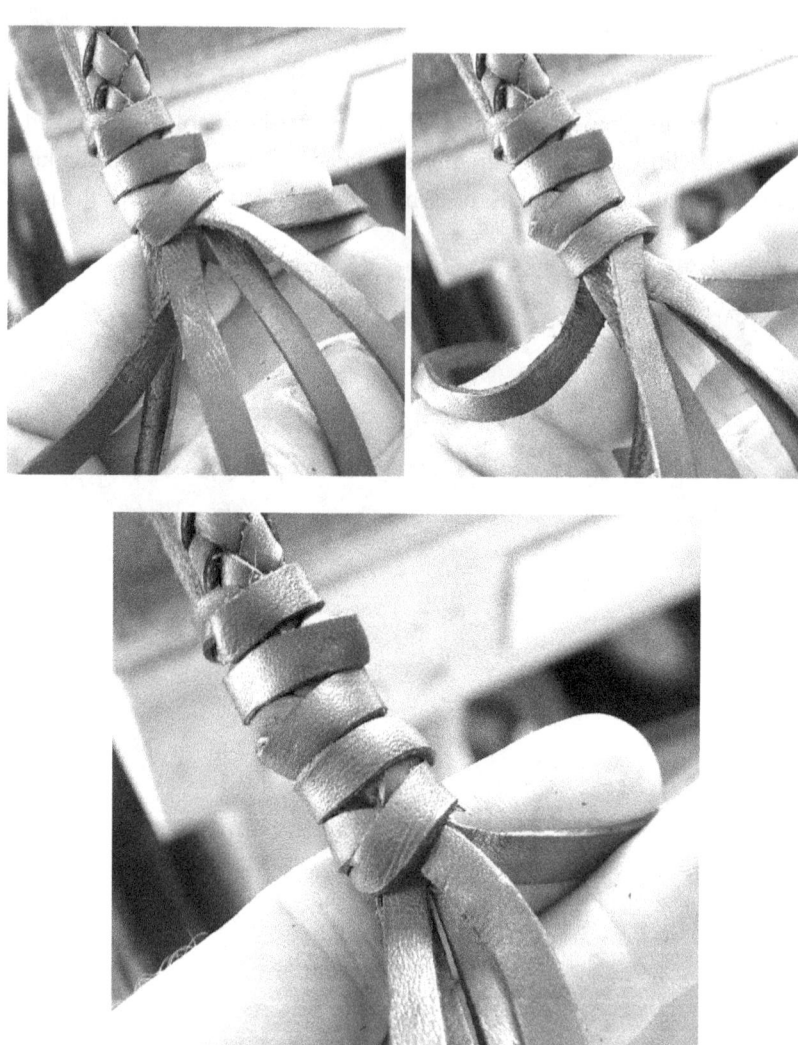

Figure 4 – take next left lace and wind round again, threading through its loop – tighten. Fig 5 – wind next right lace. Fig 6 – repeat with next left lace.

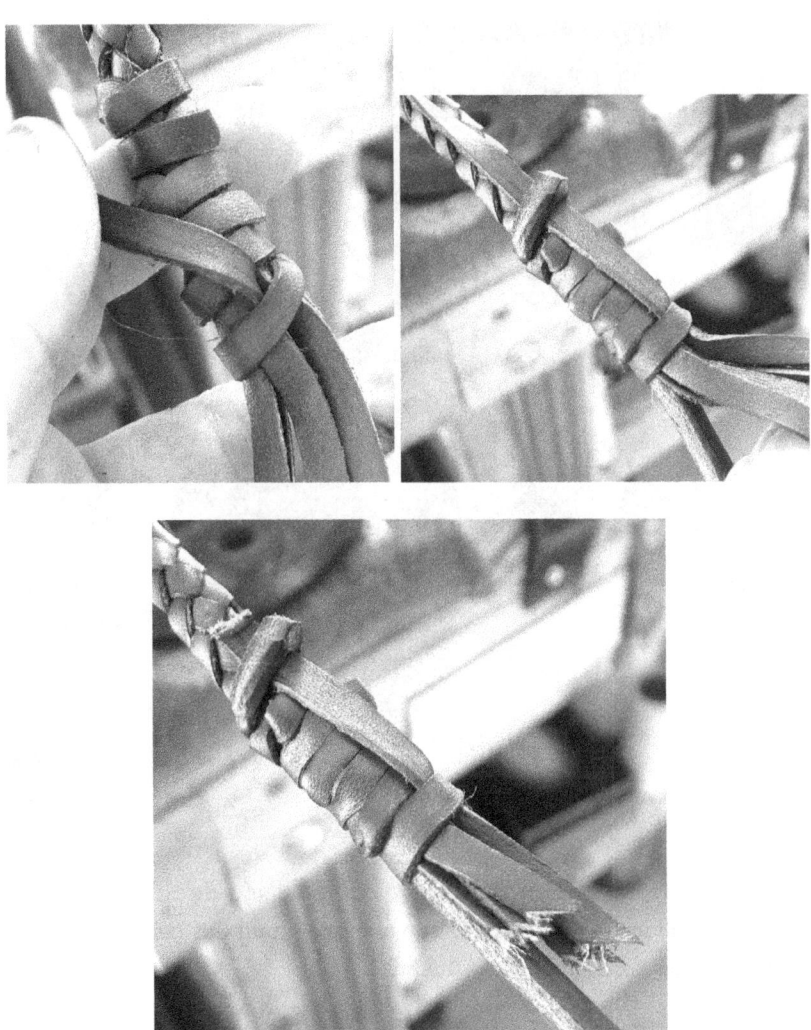

Figure 7 – with the final right hand lace, wind it around the thong and core as you have done with the five other laces, but this time thread it upwards through the loop it made and tighten. Fig 8 – tighten all the laces again with a pair of pliers if needs be, then place the upwards lace through the hole in the fall and pull the fall down. Fig 9 – Shows the fall fixed in to place and the laces cut.

Open up the end loop of the string you made and thread through the end of the fall leather and fix as shown above – pull this tight so that it is about 3 inches from the end of the fall.

Rolling the whip

In order to the roll the whip and not keep getting wacked by it, I tend to tie the fall via string onto something in order to keep it taut – the string is attached as shown.

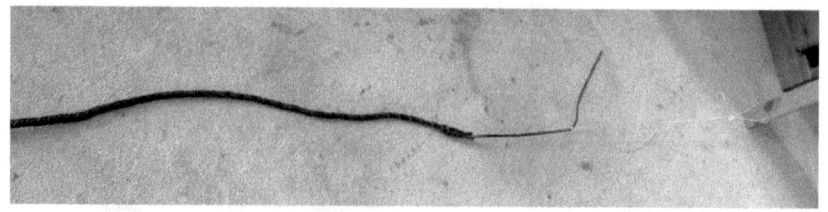

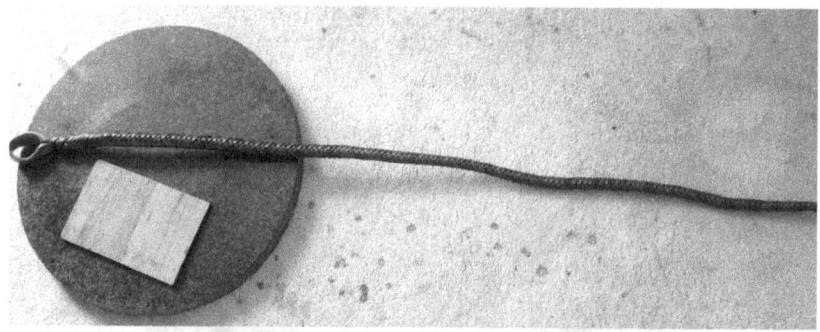

Shown above is the set up I use to roll the final inlay with it tied one end. I use a smaller block of marble which I move along as I progress along the whip thong. Doing it on the floor rather than a bench means I can put all my weight behind it when rolling. I normally roll down, then back up and down the thong again- so three times in all.

Opposite shows you the whip before and after rolling.

Transition Knot

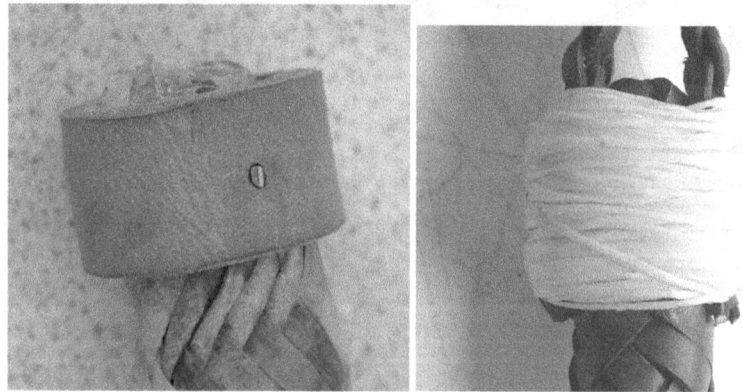

Fixing on the transition knot is just a case of sliding it up the thong onto the handle part and tighten it into place just before where the thong starts to flex. Fixing the larger top knot into place can be done in two ways; first the strap should be fixed into place about an inch in from the end of the whip and tied with artificial sinew. Then you can either 1 - measure and cut a length of 7oz leather (about 1 inch wide by circumference of whip), soak this is cold water, let dry slightly and affix with glue and nail into place with about 3 – 4 nails. Or 2 – build up the sinew already used to create the same as the leather, plus nail this also. This would be advisable if you do not have thick leather but I have found that the leather creates a better solid knot which is less likely to move with use.

After deciding on a method to fix the knot into place, slide the knot on and tighten. The left knot was fixed on top of the sinew build up, where as the right was built onto the leather. The leather does tend to create a box like knot but this can be easily remedied by skiving or edging the leather on the smooth side before fixing onto the whip.

Appendix

The following two pages have lace cutting lengths for 3ft, 5 ft, 8ft and 9ft bullwhips. These can be made following the instructions for the 6ft whip but making the 6ft first will help you understand all the sequences before going onto other lengths.

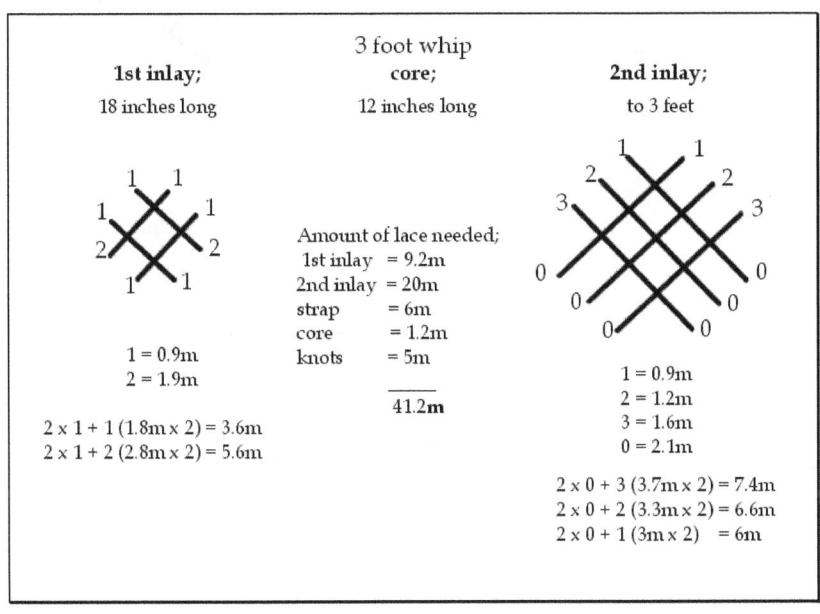

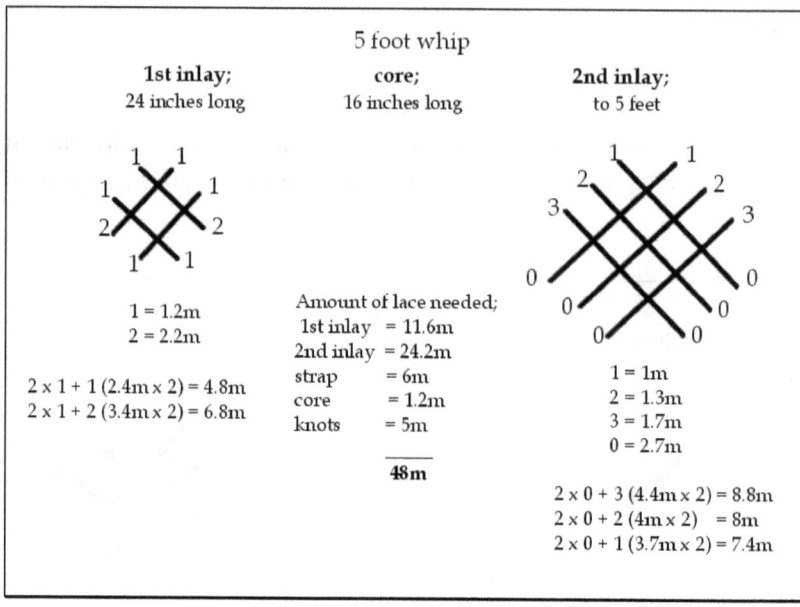

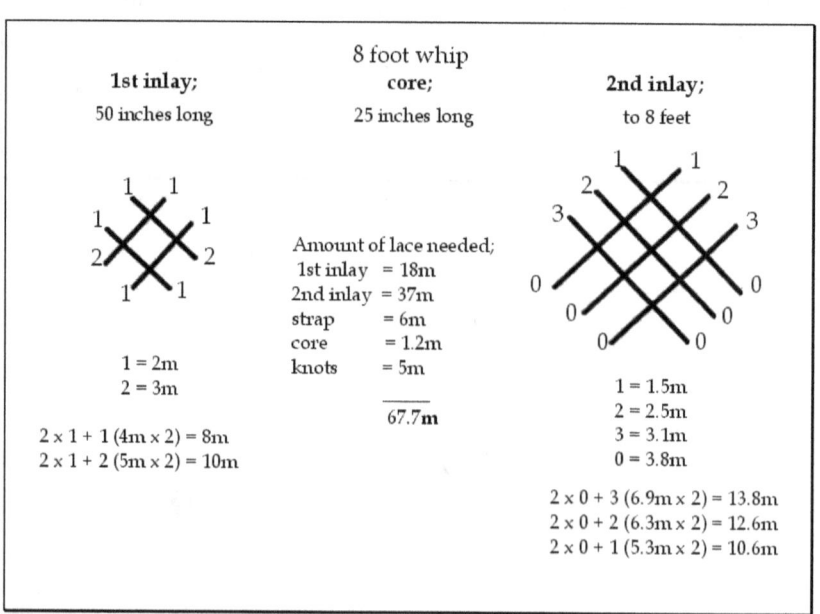

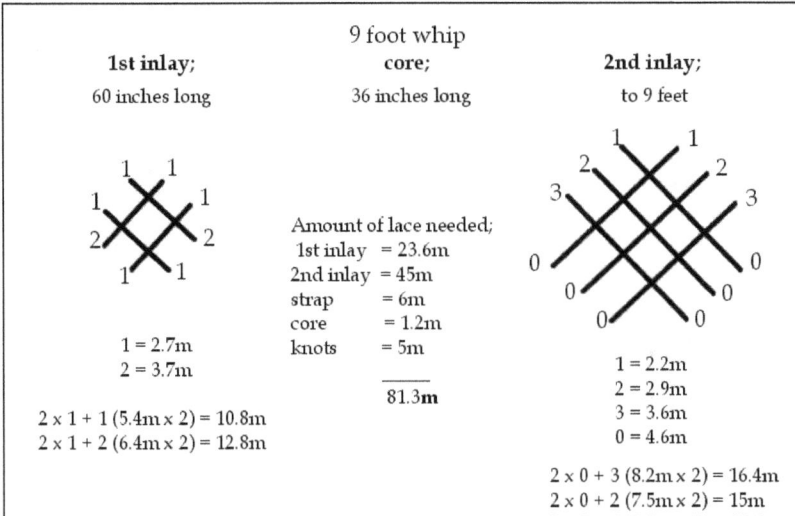

1st inlay;
60 inches long

9 foot whip core;
36 inches long

2nd inlay;
to 9 feet

1 = 2.7m
2 = 3.7m

2 x 1 + 1 (5.4m x 2) = 10.8m
2 x 1 + 2 (6.4m x 2) = 12.8m

Amount of lace needed;
1st inlay   = 23.6m
2nd inlay = 45m
strap   = 6m
core   = 1.2m
knots   = 5m
_____
81.3m

1 = 2.2m
2 = 2.9m
3 = 3.6m
0 = 4.6m

2 x 0 + 3 (8.2m x 2) = 16.4m
2 x 0 + 2 (7.5m x 2) = 15m
2 x 0 + 1 (6.8m x 2) = 13.6m

Coloured patterns for 12 lace round braid

Below are illustrated a few examples of patterns that can be created along the length of the whip thong if laces are dyed as illustrated. The small pictures are for u2, o2, u2 sequence – the larger for u3, o3. **B** = blue, **T** = green

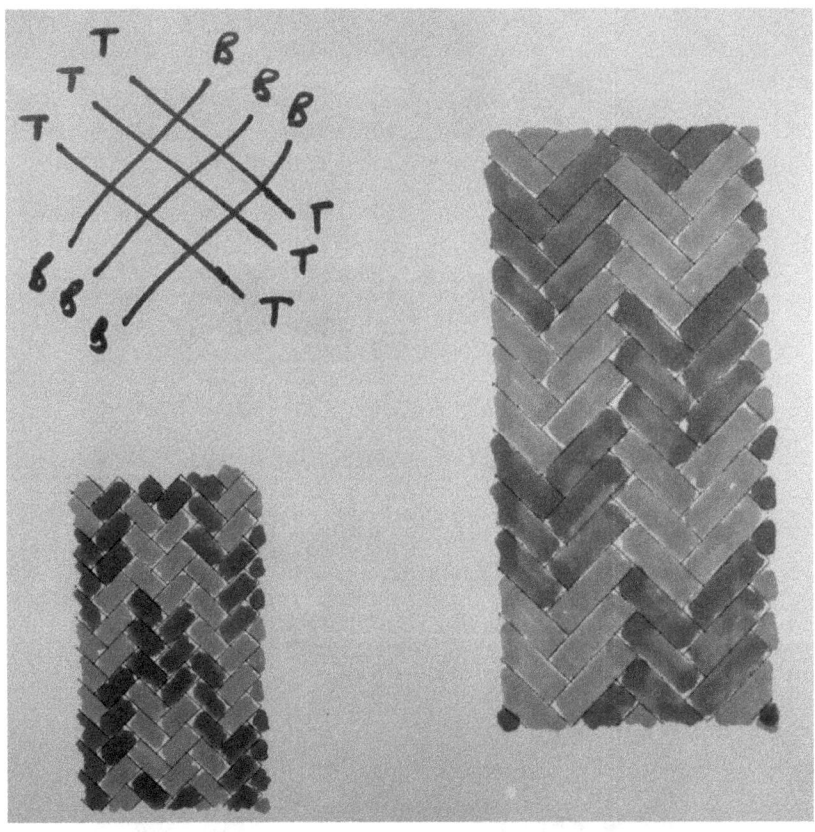

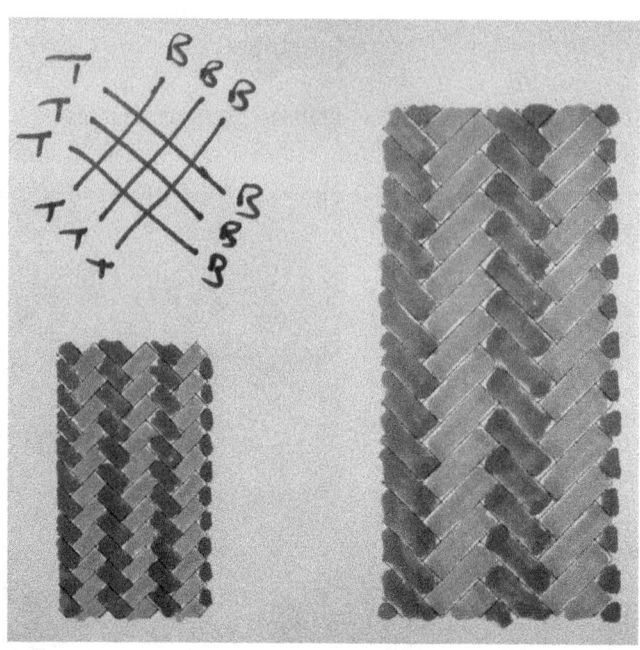
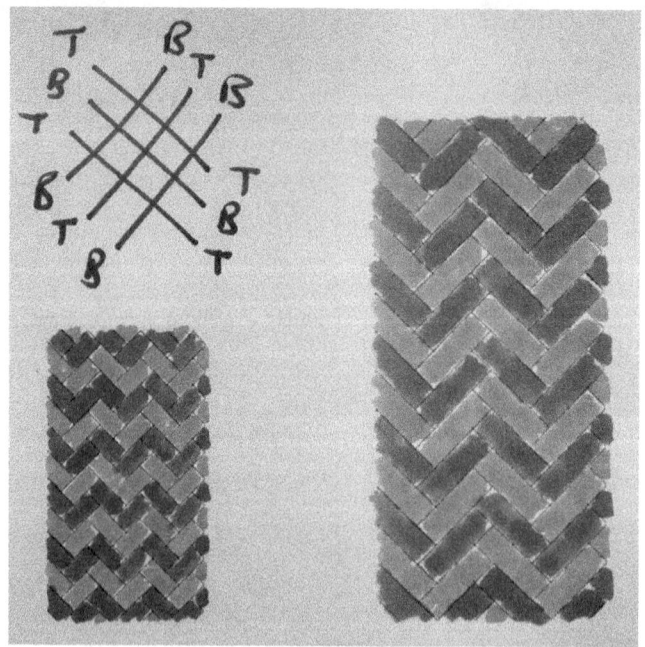

Pineapple knots

The perfect pineapple is just like the normal pineapple, i.e. it creates a knot with a herringbone pattern, but the perfect pineapple is made from only one lace whereas normally it is made up of two Turks heads interwoven together.

To help hide the ends of the fid work on this knife handle, I used two – the 9 part, 8 bights and the 13 parts, 12 bight.

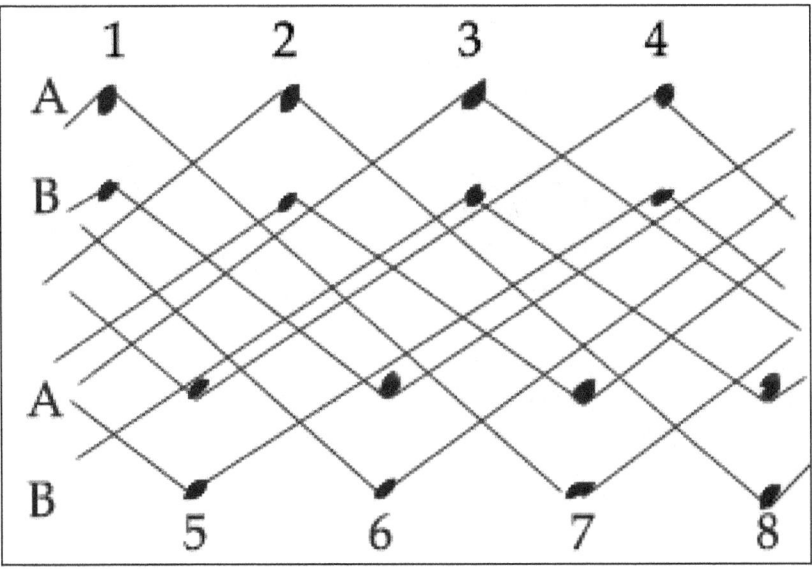

Above is a diagram of the arrangement of nails needed for the 9 part, 8 bight knot. The number of bights always indicates how many nails you need but with this knot two sets of 8 nails are needed. Please notice that the top and bottom nails are slightly off centre to one another.

Following these number above it should be easy to create this knot from the instructions below;

Up 8B   clear run   to 2A   Down
under 1   to 7A

Up 7A   clear run   to 2B   Down
over 1   to 7B

Up 7B   over 1, under 1   to 1A   Down
over 2, under 1 to 6A

Up 6A   under 2   to 1B   Down
under 1, over 2 to 6B

Up 6B   under 1, over 2, under 1   to 4A   Down   under 2,
over 2, under 1   to 5A

Up 5A   over 2, under 2   to 4B   Down   over
1, under 2, over 2   to 5B

Up 5B   over 1, under 2, over 2, under 1   to 3A   Down   over 2,
under 2, over 2, under 1   to 8A

Up 8A   under 2, over 2, under 2   to 3B   Down   under 1,
over 2, under 2, over 2   to 8B

Up 8B under 1, over 2, under 2 (do this extra to help tie off knot).

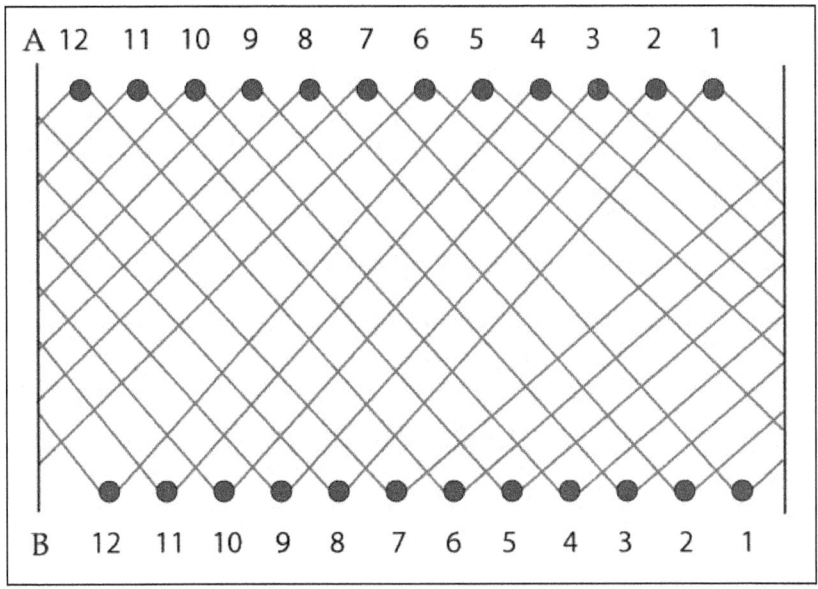

Above is the diagram for the 13 part, 12 bight knot – the only difference is that there is only two circles of nails this time instead of four

Up 1B	clear run	to 7A	Down
over 1	to 2B		
Up 2B	over 1	to 8A	Down
under 2	to 3B		
Up 3B	over 1, under 1	to 9A	Down
under 1, over 2	to 4B		
Up 4B	under 2, over 1	to 10A	Down
over 2, under 2	to 5B		
Up 5B	under 1, over 2, under 1	to 11A	Down
over 1, under 2, over 2	to 6B		

Up 6B	over 2, under 2, over 1	to 12A	Down under 2, over 2, under 2	to 7B

Up 7B	over 1, under 2, over 2, under 1	to 1A	Down	under 1, over 2, under 2, over 2	to 8B

Up 8B	under 2, over 2, under 2, over 1	to 2A	Down	over 2, under 2, over 2, under 2	to 9B

Up 9B	under 1, over 2, under 2, over 2, under 1	to 3A

Down 3A over 1, under 2, over 2, under 2, over 2	to 10B

Up 10B over 2, under 2, over 2, under 2, over 1	to 4A

Down 4A under 2, over 2, under 2, over 2, under 2 to 11B

Up 11B over 1, under 2, over 2, under 2, over 2, under 1 to 5A

Down 5A under 1, over 2, under 2, over 2, under 2,. Over 1 to 12B

Up 12B under 2, over 2, under 2, over 2, under 2, over 1 to 6A

Down 6A over 2, under 2, over 2, under 2, over 2, under 2 to 1B

Up 1B	under 1, over 2, under 2 (over the first lace to help tie the knot).

Resources

Supplies –

Ebay

Tandy – has a store in Northampton – you will need the expensive tooling double shoulders from them.

Local stone mason may sale you some marble cut off's and at a much lower price.

Books –

Ron Edwards – Bushcraft 9 – How to make whips – It's from here where I learnt alot and still do, I would regard it as a must if you wish to make whips.

Forums -

Whip basics – Forum where a few of the pro's hang out

Leatherworkers – Lots of pro leatherworkers visit here, whatever your query your find someone experienced.

APWA– An association started by Ron Edwards based in Australia and you will find alot of Pro Whipmakers here plus beginners.

You Tube – this is increasingly becoming an excellent place to find real life tutorials – put in **whip cracking – lace cutting** for starters to give you some pointers in using your new whip.

www.ingramcontent.com/pod-product-compliance
Lightning Source LLC
Chambersburg PA
LVW060405050426
819CB00009B/1904